8 Ways to Dominate Any Real Estate Market

By

Nate Martinez
Sarah Michelle Bliss

8 Ways to Dominate Any Real Estate Market

All Rights Reserved

COPYRIGHT © 2021 Nate Martinez & Sarah Michelle Bliss

This book may not be reproduced, transmitted, or stored in whole or in part by any means, including graphic, electronic, or mechanical, without the express written consent of the publisher except in the case of brief questions embodied in critical articles and reviews.

ISBN: 978-0-578-95252-9

Cover design by Orlando Diaz
Edited by Hilary Jastram

DEDICATION

This book is dedicated to our families; thank you for your unconditional love, support, and the late nights spent building this company. To the outstanding people who do and have served the team over the years, you are the heart of this book. And lastly, to the more than 1,000 REALTORS® who have come through the doors at RE/MAX Professionals, thank you for trusting in us as your mentor, teacher, coach, leader, and visionary. We would not be here today without each of you and your contributions to the PRO in RE/MAX Professionals.

RESOURCES

Website
8WaysToDominateAnyRealEstateMarket.com

FaceBook Group
facebook.com/groups/601446813632661

*Look,
if you had
one shot
or one opportunity
to seize everything you ever wanted
in one moment
Would you capture it,
or just let it slip?*

~ Eminem

CONTENTS

Dedication
Resources
Foreword
Introduction

Southwest Meets Northwest: Taking the Stairs to Success

From Newspaper Boy to Real Estate Pioneer 1
From Rags to Riches: The Red Dress of Courage 9
Arizona's Natural Resource Uses the Power of the Brand 23

Your B.H.A.G. Blueprint

What's Your Blue Dot?. 39
The Three Most Dreaded Words 47
Our Magic Pill 57
Love the Hell Out of Your Database 75
Lead-gen Like a Badass 83
Why We Celebrate Hitting Singles 99
Our Tell-all: How to Create Raving Fans 119
Accountability = Love 127

In Closing ...

The Future of Real Estate. 141

Afterword
Acknowledgments
About the Authors
Disclaimer

FOREWORD

My entire life has been blessed with amazing relationships, incredible adventures, and exceptional failures. In those experiences, I have learned that when exceptional people come into your life, you should cherish those relationships and learn from their journeys.

Nate and Sarah Michelle have been part of my life for over twenty years as we have watched each other grow, struggle, and then grow again. It has been such a pleasure to watch these incredible entrepreneurs adapt, shift, pivot, and change as the real estate industry has had many ups and downs over the last two decades.

8 Ways to Dominate Any Real Estate Market has been a labor of love as they have shared with readers their journey through the many changing conditions in the real estate market. The incredible stories and systems outlined in this book come from real-world experience, covering every aspect and every position in residential real estate. From admin to team leader from agent to mega agent to mega team leader and now, owner of multiple offices, Nate and Sarah Michelle have shared their unique perspectives eloquently and precisely. It is rare to find two people with so much knowledge and experience who are willing to pull the covers back (so to speak) and share what really works and what doesn't in business. Their insight and attitudes are contagious as they share very clearly how to succeed in any type of real estate market.

Nate and his partner have hired me several times over the years to speak, train and coach their top performers, and I have had the opportunity to coach Nate as he transitioned back from selling hundreds of bank-owned properties to selling traditional listings and high-end homes in gated communities. His work ethic, marketing skills, and sheer desire to succeed have been impressive to watch and an honor to be part of.

Both Nate and Sarah Michelle are Master Coaches at Workman Success and continue to share their insights and experience with others as they continue to run their successful businesses. It is a great honor and very difficult to become a Master Coach because of the time, understanding of business principles, and that you must have a success-based track record with clients. They are truly masters in helping others grow both personally and professionally.

As one of the most respected broker-owners of RE/MAX franchises in the world, Nate uses his influence to affect real change in one of the most powerful brands in the world. Walking through the halls at a RE/MAX conference with Nate is like hanging out with a rock star.

He has made such an impact on brokers, owners, agents, and team leaders simply by sharing what works and what doesn't. It's cool to see all the love that surrounds him. As a father, it has been great to watch him bring his family into the business and really develop and allow them to grow in the business he loves so much.

As you take this journey, you will see that as a leader, Nate has great vision and an uncanny ability to create an environment that allows him to realize his grand plans and goals.

Sarah Michelle is unique as she started out as a buyer's agent on Nate's team, grew to be a top producer on the team, and then transitioned to a supporting role in real estate as the team leader (while continuing to sell). Her insights into the industry come from being in the business and working at every level. She sees what must be done through an operation's lens and applies systems to everything she does. It's like watching a great artist paint a masterpiece when Sarah Michelle gets a hold of something she is passionate about and puts all the pieces together—whether it's in her business, one of Nate's businesses, or as a Master Coach.

The best advice I can give to those who are lucky enough to read this book is to just get into it.

Live in curiosity, and you will find great nuggets of gold and a clear road map to success in your business and your life.

You will be blown away by their honesty and vulnerability as they open up their lives and businesses to help you find your own path to success through their eight simple steps.

My sincere gratitude goes out to Nate and Sarah Michelle and their families for sharing with us their journeys. I can't wait to see what the future holds for these rock stars of real estate, and I am honored to be part of their journey.

Verl Workman
Founder/CEO
Workman Success Systems

INTRODUCTION

*E*veryone who enters the workforce makes a decision about who they want to be while they're on the job. Some don't really care, and they tend to find themselves jumping from company to company—often involuntarily—and leaving no imprint anywhere. Others are fine with doing acceptable work and flying under the radar, but after a while, that can lead to boredom, apathy, and complacency.

A third type of person, however, wants more from their career. They bring their A game every day. I like to say they have "fire in their belly." They refuse to coast, they focus on serving others, they stand out, and they often have decades of success. These people make a real difference in their company and in the lives of people around them.

Two such individuals wrote the book you're reading now.

I've known Nate Martinez for many years. Fact is, it would be impossible to lead RE/MAX and not know him because Nate isn't a fly-under-the-radar kind of guy. He's as active and involved as they come.

Just as dynamic is Sarah Michelle Bliss, a popular coach, and educator in her own right. Since 1997, she's worked alongside Nate to shape and lead one of the most successful RE/MAX operations in existence.

The Nate Martinez Team's 30-year history at RE/MAX is the story of going all-in on real estate as a career and RE/MAX as a brand. It's also a story of hustle, struggle, change, innovation, coachability, resilience, action, and sustained excellence.

But – because of who Nate and Sarah Michelle are—this book isn't about their success. It's about yours.

In *8 Ways to Dominate Any Real Estate Market*, they're sharing the blueprint that took them to the highest levels of our industry. They're sharing their strategies, tactics, secrets, insights—and yes, even their stumbles—to help you on your own real estate journey.

Why?

Because they understand the value of giving and the enormous satisfaction of helping other people succeed. They're saying, "We accomplished this, and you can, too."

Several references to Nate and Sarah Michelle's friend and coach, the late, great Howard Brinton, suggest that by helping you, they're also paying back the colleagues and mentors who helped them along the way. It underscores one of the book's many themes: that when you surround yourself with positive, productive, passionate people, you position yourself to be influenced in that same direction. That's a recipe for success in any field.

Although the ideas shared in this book are invaluable, readers will also realize how bumpy the road can be. Nate and Sarah both give honest, sometimes uncomfortable accounts of the struggles they faced in their early years, and they also relate the many challenges and setbacks they encountered later—even when things were going well.

What I take away from these parts is that mindset and attitude—perhaps more than anything else—can lift you past any obstacles.

You might be dealing with personal issues. Market turns. Competitive threats. But any of them can be overcome by drive and determination. Your coaches, mentors, and leaders can give you the roadmap—as will this book—but your success ultimately comes down to you and the way you approach the daily demands of the business.

One word both Nate and Sarah Michelle use frequently is "intentional." They're intentional with their time, intentional with their budgeting, intentional with their choices. Do they still take risks and leaps of faith? Sure. But they're intentional even when doing that. In a business where many newcomers focus more on shiny objects like online lead generation and not enough on cultivating referrals through relationships, Nate, and Sarah Michelle outline specific, strategic—intentional—business-building steps to take with people you already know. In doing so, they provide a starting point that has launched or recharged countless top producers.

So, regardless of where you are in your real estate career, *8 Ways to Dominate Any Real Estate Market* outlines a time-tested path for you.

People who don't care all that much, well … they're not even aware of this book, let alone interested in reading it. Others who are fine with being part of the pack will benefit from the ideas being shared, and they might even be inspired to change their course.

But this book is really for the people who want to soar, who want to stand out, to make a difference … to impact as many lives as possible—that's who Nate and Sarah Michelle are speaking to in the pages that follow.

If that sounds like you, dig in. And, when you're done, by all means, take action. This just might be the start of your own journey to incredible heights.

Dave Liniger
Chairman and Co-Founder
RE/MAX Holdings, Inc.

Southwest Meets Northwest: Taking the Stairs to Success

NATE ...

- 1 -
From Newspaper Boy to Real Estate Pioneer

"I skate to where the puck is going to be, not to where it has been."

~ Wayne Gretzky

When I was a little kid, I was plagued with a fear of not having enough … even though we had nothing.

My mom was extremely frugal, and I can remember watching her take her weekly paycheck and divide the money into separate envelopes. There was an envelope for groceries, utilities, rent, etc. She was doing the Dave Ramsey system 50+ years ago. I also remember picking up on the vibe that there wasn't enough, and this system my mom had for money was the only way she managed to pay the bills each month.

Before the age of ten, I started having this dream that when I walked into our living room, I would see stacks and stacks of bundled cash lined against the wall from floor to ceiling. It was like something you'd see in a drug house movie scene. I can see this image very clearly in my mind's eye, even today. I believe this vision and the deeply rooted fear of not having enough is what caused me to be so driven to achieve more, even though I had no idea what "more" was because I had never been exposed to anything else.

It might sound odd, but I didn't know we were poor, despite our circumstances.

Our family didn't have much money, and our world was very limited. Back then, there was no internet, and my mom, a single parent, worked long, hard hours just to make ends sort of meet.

Some nights, I would wake up in an anxiety attack over money. It was like a compounding debt scenario—if I lost one penny, I would be worried about how to get it back two-fold.

My siblings were older than me and out of the house, which meant I was on my own. I can remember thinking that if everyone in my family died, I'd be left with the bills, and there would be no money. It was up to me to make my own future, even if that meant doing some shady shit.

Something in my gut told me there was more to life.

I guess that's what led me to start working at a young age, throwing newspapers. Later I became a bagger at the local grocery store. Eventually, that job led to my first management position.

We lived in the inner-city on the west side of Phoenix in an area known as Maryvale—however, I knew it as "Hollywood" —the street name. Like most inner cities, there were plenty of drugs, gangs, and opportunities to get into trouble. As horrible as this sounds (and feels to write), drugs were easy, and selling them was a way out of poverty and the daily struggle to survive.

To make matters weirder, I looked up to people with money. In my neighborhood, they were the drug dealers. And they were also the mentors in the hood.

Many of my friends were arrested and sent to jail at some point—some were gunned down and murdered. I went to high school with a guy I called "Mr. GQ" because he was unfairly good-looking with the long, lustrous flowing hair and chiseled jawline of a model on the cover of **GQ Magazine.** And, of course, he had a super-hot girlfriend to go along with his super good looks. He had it all going on, including being one of "Hollywood's" favorite drug dealers. Sadly, Mr. GQ was shot in the parking lot of a grocery store in the hood when a drug deal went bad.

Then there is the story of another "Hollywood" drug dealer who was murdered in his home after someone found out about his "stash and cash" (which, if you don't know, "stash" is street terminology for drugs).

Or there is the story of the "thug" in the gang. He was not someone you wanted to mess with, but his untimely death came when he was machine-gunned down in his front yard over a gang-related conflict.

Due to my associations, I had my share of opportunities to get into trouble with the law, but I was lucky because even though the path I was on was taking me nowhere good, I knew I had a choice to make.

I could stay in the hood and get deeper into trouble with the law, or worse, get murdered—or I could leave.

So, at seventeen, my girlfriend and I moved into an apartment about three miles away, which I believed was "outside" of my hood. I was forced to become a man then, but in hindsight, it was my second chance at a better life.

After my car got broken into at that apartment, I decided to buy a house – my first house at only seventeen years old. It was a two-bedroom, two-bath that needed to be finished, but I managed to get a loan with no qualification and $5,000 down. We finished it, and a year later, at eighteen years old, I sold that house and bought my next house. Looking back, I can see that this drive to be a homeowner then was the start of something incredible, even though I didn't know it at the time.

I can remember sitting on the patio of my second home off 54th Ave and McDowell in Phoenix, writing in a Tony Robbins' journal I bought after watching one of his late-night TV infomercials. I didn't know anything about setting goals or the power of intention by writing them down; I just knew I wanted something more for my life and the life of my family. And everything I wrote down came true, including buying a home in a nicer community so my daughter could go to a better school and purchasing a home for my mother-in-law.

My mom wanted me to become an engineer because that was the career field my biological dad (who I never knew) had chosen, so I started taking mechanical engineering classes at Phoenix Community College.

It was a tough life to juggle since I was not yet an adult and was going to school and working full-time. In the second semester, I really struggled with English class and had no confidence when it came to public speaking. I couldn't even deliver a five-minute speech to twenty-eight kids in my class. It was a 6:00 pm class, and I showed up. But as I put my hand on the doorknob to the classroom, I was gripped with a terrifying fear, and I just couldn't turn the knob. So, I left and never went back. That was the day I quit college.

Instead, I focused on my job at Safeway, a grocery store in the Valley of the Sun. I begged the district manager to allow me to work at two different store locations for two different managers—I was that hungry to make ends meet so we could have a better life.

Fast forward to 1981, ten days before my twenty-second birthday. By then, my first child, Brandi, had been born.

The streets were still trying to pull me in. I was facing the choice of being in one of two gangs. The gangbangers running the streets, or a tribe of brothers who shared a passion for lowrider cars—which is how I formed the car club, Malo.

I chose the car club scene because it was organized and positive—and at least we had jobs and cars! The club wasn't about fighting another gang or neighborhood boundaries; it was about having a nice car and cruisin' Central Avenue on a Friday night. Eventually, Malo merged with Spirit Car Club, and it's now one of the most recognized car clubs in the world.

In reflecting on that time in my life, I can clearly see the dots connecting what was to be my future. Bringing Malo and Spirit Car Clubs together as one entity was my first business merger, which at the time, I didn't realize, but this was a critical point in my life and would later help me as I have done several mergers and acquisitions in my real estate career.

Spirit was far more organized and sophisticated than my club. They had rules and bylaws. If you wanted to be a part of Spirit, your car had to be cherry, and you had to adhere to the rules of the club. We did good things in the community, like charity work, and made appearances at events. We even made it to the Fiesta Bowl Parade!

The club made money by appearing at car shows, or people would pay us to make an appearance at a party like a quinceañera (an elaborate Hispanic celebration that occurs when a female child turns fifteen). The Spirit Car Club was the baddest car club in town. For the first time in my life, I was proud of what I was doing.

Even though a lot of good was happening with the car club, I was still surrounded by drugs and crime. I remember being at a local car shop with the owner when our buddy came skidding into the parking lot in his tricked-out lowrider Caddie.

He opened the driver's side door and toppled onto the ground with blood gushing from his side. The quarter panel of his car had a golf-ball-size shotgun hole through it, and the interior of the car was full of shredded insulation from the inside of the car door. He had been involved in a high-speed chase with a rival car club, and they had managed to shoot him through the side of his Cadillac while racing down the freeway.

We scooped up my friend, and I drove him to the emergency room at St. Joseph's Hospital in Phoenix, where, fortunately, they saved his life.

People say you are the sum of the five people you spend the most time with, and even though I loved the car club, I needed to change who I was hanging out with to truly change my life.

During that time, I started to really question what else was out there—there had to be more to life than drugs, murder, and rivals—especially for my baby girl, Brandi. I didn't want her growing up in the hood or thinking it was normal to hear random gunshots in the middle of the night. She was my motivation to get out of "Hollywood" and create a better life for all of us.

I look back at that time and my decision to start the Malo car club, and I can see that it helped me to develop a leadership skill—which has been a crucial part of my success.

Also crucial to my success has been my ability to always connect with people fairly easily. Luckily, I have been blessed with good people in my life. Combining that with my enhanced leadership skills, crystal-clear vision, and insatiable drive for a better life has allowed me to create a legacy in my real estate business.

Since 1986, I have had the pleasure of working with some of the best agents in our industry and have assisted in the development of dozens of agents on my team and in my brokerage. I have been fortunate enough to own multiple office locations and serve with the local Arizona Association of REALTORS®, the National Association of REALTORS®, as well as to hold the position of president of the Phoenix Association of REALTORS®. My team has helped more than 6,000 families buy or sell a home in the Valley of the Sun, and the agents who work at RE/MAX Professionals consistently close more than 3,000 transactions per year.

Getting to this point took a lot of hard work and hustle. It required long days and plenty of missed dinners to build up my business to where it is today. In the late 1980s and early 1990s, we were selling HUD homes on the court steps in downtown Phoenix for $15,000, $20,000, and $30,000. (We used to call them "scratch and sniffs" because I thought you ought to be able to smell them first before you bought them!) If you do the math, you'll find you have to move a lot of real estate at those prices to make a decent living.

For the first few years of my real estate career, I worked full-time pouring concrete, then busted my ass in the evenings and on the weekends selling properties. I had a new wife, a young child, and the concrete job provided security and benefits for my family. But as my real estate business started to grow, so did my confidence.

I took my then-wife on the honeymoon we'd never had, which was my first trip to Hawaii. It was on the sandy beach of beautiful Maui that I made the decision to quit the construction job. I told my wife at the time that I was going to quit, then put it out to the universe. When we returned from Hawaii, I followed through with that commitment, and it was the best decision of my life.

If I look back at all the trials, tribulations, risks, and opportunities—time seems like it hardly moved. But forty years ago, I was sitting in a jail cell.

In making the decision to stick to my promise, I broke the mold, not only for me but for my children, their children, and their children. Today, I have the pleasure of working alongside my two adult children, Brandi, and Nate Jr., as well as my better half Tonya. Getting to see my children thrive in the very industry that changed our lives is a feeling I can't describe in words.

The life I get to live now all came about because I made the decision to become a REALTOR®. It's been absolutely mind-blowingly amazing! And it's my hope that by sharing my story—my career, what worked, what didn't, how I owed the IRS, got divorced, managed a team, struggled as a father, owned a multi-office brokerage—and all the guts and glory, that you will be inspired and motivated to live a life by design that makes you want to jump out of bed every day.

Every day I wake up with the knowledge that this is the greatest industry and the best job in the world. I can't wait to get up and go to work. I want you to feel that way, too.

SARAH …

- 2 -
From Rags to Riches: The Red Dress of Courage

"What lies behind us and what lies before us are small matters compared to what lies within us."

~ Ralph Waldo Emerson

I was born in 1976 in central Oregon and spent the first nine years of my life bouncing from one town to the next, depending on the job my dad had at the time.

He wasn't good at staying employed, so my large family always lacked money, and my parents constantly fought over it.

While I knew we were poor, I was still the eternal optimist as I believed, no matter how hard we had it, some little girl out there in the world had it worse off than me.

Today, I can look back on that little girl with the "glass is half full" attitude and know that belief helped me survive the physical and mental abuse that was "reality" in my home.

Just before I turned ten, my parents separated, and it took what felt like forever for their divorce to finalize. My life was turned upside down like someone had taken a snow globe and shook it a thousand times. My mother, who had been a stay-at-home parent, went to work to pay the bills.

After my parents split, we had visitation with my dad every other weekend. It was a time of uncertainty, turmoil, and heartbreak, but I remained the optimist because I knew that someday I would grow up and have a better life. I would not be poor and live in a trailer ever again.

In 1994, two months before I graduated high school, I got married to a man who was significantly older than me. My then-sister-in-law was dating a guy who happened to be a REALTOR®. He got me my first job in real estate as a receptionist for a boutique brokerage in Scottsdale, Arizona, in 1995.

Part of my job included updating the MLS (Multiple Listing Service) book each day when the Phoenix Association of REALTORS® would fax over the new listings, price changes, and status changes. Boy, have we come a long way with technology!

During my training, I was told that the receptionist needed to celebrate the agents' wins and pick them up during their lows. If they had a deal fall apart, the rest of the admins and I were the cheerleaders to make them feel like everything would be okay.

I will never forget the sweet little old lady, Jeannie King, who worked for the brokerage. She was elegant and beautiful, dripping in jewels and fur coats with perfectly groomed hair and manicured nails—a true class act and the epitome of "Scottsdale."

She would gracefully float into the office and to the bullpen area, where we had the big grease board on the wall. Then she would write her newest sales up on the board and ring the bell to celebrate her success. Everyone in the office would cheer for her, and then, brick cellphones in tow, they would head off to lunch in her Cadillac.

That's what I thought real estate was when I first got into the business. *I get a brick cellphone, a fancy car, a fur coat, some diamonds, and I can ring the bell.*☺

I quickly worked my way up from the front desk to the back office, where I eventually audited broker files and trained agents on writing contracts, addendums, and disclosures properly. One day, I handed a $10,000 commission check to an agent I had trained, and that's when I realized I was on the wrong side of that exchange. It was time to get my real estate license.

At this point, my marriage was beginning to fail, and I knew it was only a matter of time before I would be divorced. But I did not have a pot to piss in, let alone a window to throw it out of (the house was in his name). I was also suffering from debilitating depression brought on by childhood baggage and the looming decision that I was not happy in my marriage, but I had nothing and no way to support myself. I did, however, have a real estate license and a $3,000 Citibank Credit Card.

One night after a group therapy session for children of codependency, I reached a breaking point. Sitting in a circle among a group of women much older than me who were depressed, miserable, and wasting away their lives living with their childhood trauma, I thought there had to be more to life. There had to be a way to be happy.

When I got home that evening, I phoned my boss and quit. This led to a nasty fight with my ex-husband; he was mad that I'd spent money on real estate school and even angrier that I had quit my job with no fallback plan. He went on to remind me of what my mother used to say to me growing up: "You'll always be a loser just like your dad."

While that was a horrible thing to say to me, I am actually grateful he said it. Those words lit a fire inside me to prove him—and my mom wrong. I remembered I had made a vow to myself as a little girl that I'd be different, that I'd rise above the poverty, abuse, and dysfunction. *F*ck what they said! I was not a loser.*

The very next day, I started making phone calls to real estate offices near my home. Since I had all the admin experience, understood the contract language, the contingency periods, and how the general purchase process went, I thought I could find a job as a transaction coordinator.

I made a phone call to the RE/MAX office up the street and spoke to the Designated Broker, Ed McCloud. He told me that they were not hiring; however, Nate Martinez was always looking for buyer's agents.

I knew who Nate was.

A few weeks prior, I had competed against him for a listing. When I saw all his beautiful marketing samples lying on the seller's kitchen table, I thought to myself; *I'd list my house with Nate, too!* His signs were everywhere, and he was well-known in the area.

I didn't know what a buyer's agent was, but I was on a mission and needed money to get a place of my own and file for divorce. That was 1997, and while I was prepping to meet with Nate, I had interviewed with a commercial broker who had offered me a $50,000 salary to be his right hand. That was a mind-blowing amount of money for a trailer-park girl like me.

I will never forget the day I interviewed with Nate.

I was only twenty years old with braces and big glasses, which made me look like I was fifteen. My one business suit which I had bought at a "Rags to Riches" event (rich people donated their clothes which were sold at a steep discount to people like me) was a red wool business jacket and skirt with big shoulder pads and huge, gaudy gold buttons. It was wool and a horrible choice for Arizona heat. But this red dress gave me confidence, which I desperately needed to come across like I was credible, capable, and not a hot mess with baggage and a bad marriage.

Nate was late for our appointment. When he arrived, he arrogantly put his feet up on the conference room table and asked me one question that changed my life: "Are you hungry?" I think my response went something like, "You have no idea!"

He didn't want to hire me because I was too young and green. But I wouldn't go away. The week of my initial interview, Nate was helping to host a real estate conference in downtown Phoenix with his mentor Howard Brinton and a bunch of other "stars" who were big-time agents (you might remember Howard and his amazing Star Power organization). Nate was one of those "star" agents.

During our interview, Nate suggested with a dash of sarcasm that I should attend. I don't think he thought I would put in the effort to show up to an event where I knew no one, surrounded by top dogs in the industry—and all the way downtown (parking can be a real bitch!).

Truth be told, I was down to my last few bucks in the bank, and the idea of spending five of those precious dollars on parking for a 1099 job that I had no clue I would get was painful and terrifying. I knew in my gut that this was a test to see if I had the fire in my belly. So, I went and spent the five dollars on parking—it was a gamble, but I was all-in.

I don't remember if I actually saw Nate that day at the conference, but I did end up finding his team and, most importantly, his office manager, who later became one of my dearest friends during the years we were teammates. The word got back to Nate that I was there, and when I followed up with a phone call the next day, I was invited to attend a meeting where I would be interviewed by the other team members and given a personality assessment known as DISC. This felt like another huge hurdle to jump, and it kind of was. This was the number one team in the RE/MAX Southwest Region; not just anyone could join without a few hurdles to jump over.

I could easily have taken the salaried job with the commercial agent and probably would have had a great life, too. But a feeling in my gut pulled me to the job with Nate with no salary and no guarantee, and I would even be required to pay a monthly desk fee. Taking it was a giant risk and required that I take a huge leap of faith into the unknown, but I knew with every fiber of my being, it was the right decision.

Twenty-four years later … I am so grateful that I took the risk and banked on the opportunity to be a part of the best real estate team in Arizona. Without a doubt, I would do it over again. I cannot imagine my life any other way.

On December 7, 1997, I joined Nate's Team as a newbie buyer's agent. He gave me a book (that I still have) called ***30 Days to Success in Real Estate*** by Dianna Kokoszka, Tony DiCello, and Howard Brinton Seminars, Inc. When Nate handed it to me, our conversation went something like this:

Nate: "Do you trust me?"

Me: (Blinking hard before answering), "Yes."

Nate: "If I told you that standing on the corner in a chicken suit would make you money, would you do it?"

Me: (Blinking even harder and thinking I didn't look good in yellow, but a girl's gotta do what a girl's gotta do), "Yes!"

Nate: "Good. Now take this book and do everything it says to do over the next thirty days."

Me: (Gulp) "Okay."

Day One: Buy an index card holder and cards. Write the names, addresses, and phone numbers of every person you know on the index cards. Then start calling them.

Pretty old school, but it worked…and it still works.

Also, in this "30 days to success," paperback spiral-bound book of real estate gold nuggets was an exercise called the Quantum Leap. The instruction was to visualize a goal you wanted to achieve for ten minutes every day, twice a day preferred, either in your mind's eye or if you had a photo, even better. At the time, I wanted to purchase a newer Jet Ski for my then-husband. We had one already, which we loved, and I wanted a second one that was better and newer for him.

The instructions in the Quantum Leap tell you to get super specific with the details. To imagine the sun on your face as you glide across the water, the smell of the sunblock on your skin, to feel the water spraying you as you accelerate. It asks you questions like, who are you with? What are you talking about? What are you eating? What part of the lake are you spending the day at?

You are also advised to hear your own voice laughing with joy. Every day, for ten minutes.

Then you are to spend two minutes writing down what it felt like to have achieved the goal. Upon conclusion of the two minutes of journaling, I was to write this passage: "I am making the Quantum Leap. I know exactly where I am going, and I am open to the unexpected."

I had never heard of anything like this, but I told Nate I trusted him, and he had gifted me with this book that was supposed to change my life. So, I did it. Every. Single. Day.

Proudly, I can tell you that in April 1998, I bought that exact Jet Ski that I had a photo of hanging on my refrigerator—for cash. It was the same make and same model even. That picture was my visual guide.

The Quantum Leap worked! And I still use it to this day. #GAMECHANGER

I was the first buyer's agent in the office most days and the last to leave. When I would come home at night, both my younger brother, who lived with us at the time and my ex-husband would ask me if I had sold a house that day.

I looked forward to the days when I could happily say, "YES!" It fueled me to keep going on the many days I hadn't sold a house. I don't think they realized the accountability they were providing just by asking a silly question at the end of my day. But it was motivating because I wanted more than anything for them to be proud of me.

In my first year selling real estate, I outperformed Nate's top dog buyer's agent and was just shy of making "Rookie of the Year" for the Phoenix Association of REALTORS®. *And* I went five months without getting a paycheck. Then in April, I finally had something to show for all my hard work and deposited over $10,000 in our bank account. For a girl like me, who grew up often wondering what we'd have to eat besides bread and water, this was a huge amount of money and certainly more than I'd ever imagined I could make.

I couldn't wait to get home and show my ex-husband the deposit slip. He was in the driveway with my brother working on his car. I hopped out of my SUV, super excited to share my accomplishment; unfortunately, it was not the moment I had played out in my mind.

He took the slip of paper, glared at it with disgust, and said, "That's it? We've been starving for months, and that is all you have to show for yourself?" I don't need to write what my two-word response was, but it's universally understood.

Despite his disappointment in my commission, my ex-husband went on to spend every penny that I had earned in less than a month. I was shocked and confused because, at that time, we were living a very modest life, and $10,000 should have been six months of what we needed to pay bills.

That's when I dug into our finances and discovered we were $32,000 in the hole in credit card debt. (Remember, this was in 1997, so that was a really big number in my mind.)

I talked to Nate about the situation, and he gave me this advice: "If you are going to get a divorce, do it before you make any more money in real estate."

I moved out on July 2, 1998, and we were divorced about a year later.

Fast forward to 2001 …

Nate had a need for a manager to help him run the day-to-day functions of his business. By that time, I had already established myself as a leader amongst my teammates. I moved into the role of "team manager" and continued to sell real estate. We lived through the dot.com/dot-bomb period, 911, the boom of investors, the short sale wave, the REO (REO stands for real-estate owned, and it is a property that has been foreclosed on by the bank.) market, and now, we are back to what is a more traditional market.

During the boom, there were three buyer's agents on the team and three admins. It was March of 2003, and I was working with a first-time buyer named Rachel. That's when I found myself in unchartered waters, as every property we looked at had multiple offers. It took several contracts before we could secure an accepted offer for her. I had never experienced a situation like this, and it was just the beginning.

I don't need to tell you about what happened next, but that was the day when everything started to change. Not too long after that, Nate got a phone call from a guy representing an investment group in the California Bay Area. He wanted to purchase real estate in the Valley of the Sun. Nate agreed to meet with him, and that phone call resulted in our team selling 380 homes to this group of investors. (This story is a good reminder to answer your phone!)

When you hear the stories about Californians coming in busloads to Arizona, it isn't too far from the truth.

These folks had cashed out the equity in their California homes with the intention of buying up the "cheap" real estate in Phoenix to turn into rental properties. They leveraged that money to buy multiple properties at the same time and financed them with adjustable-rate loans—with no clue about what would happen in a few years—when those rates adjusted.

We were being presented with an opportunity to move a lot of real estate; however, there was a catch. These investors wanted half the commission, and our buyers' agents were on a 50/50 split. That meant we had to do a lot of work with a significantly smaller paycheck.

Before we made the decision of which way we would go, the whole team met in the conference room to map it out on paper. After hashing it over, we agreed to a team goal of selling 300 units that year. The reward would be a team trip to Cancun.

My favorite moment that day happened when the team and I stood around the conference room table. Each of us put our hands in a circle as we made the commitment to reach our goals together. Then we collectively shouted, "Go, Team!" That year we sold 325 homes and spent a week in beautiful Cancun.

My least favorite memories on my team followed the boom, but as you will read about in the next chapter, the decision to work the REO market might be the very reason I am still in the industry. It might be the very decision I can write this book for you.

At one point, we had eighteen people on the team; six were field inspectors. One person was dedicated to solely preparing BPOs (broker price opinions); we had multiple listing managers and transaction managers. My job was to negotiate all the offers. In 2008 I calculated that I had negotiated over 2,000 offers for the 679 units we'd sold.

We had accounts with Freddie Mac, Fannie Mae, Wells Fargo, and several other smaller REO companies. A very systematized machine was required to handle the sheer volume of new assignments coming in daily. We managed evictions, cash for keys, property checks, utilities, etc., and called ourselves the "friendly REO team." This name was just as much of a reminder to each of us on the team to be kind, patient, and understanding with each other as it was to be kind to other agents, asset managers, and the public.

We went as far as creating a form for each REO account with detailed, step-by-step instructions on how to write an offer specific to that bank's requirements. And we set up a phone system that provided recorded information on which properties had offers in negotiations, which were available, and any other important details to help the agents in our market. At the peak, we had several hundred for sale signs in the yards of foreclosed properties across the Valley. To say the volume of incoming calls was taxing is an understatement!

Mondays were the worst. We would come into a few dozen new foreclosure assignments, and some properties would receive as many as 30-50 offers! Our running joke was that the staff needed catheters and feeding tubes because there was no time to use the restroom or take a break to eat lunch! Even worse were the days when a buyer who had been beaten out multiple times, desperate to buy a home, would get my cell phone number and call me crying or screaming in frustration.

But far worse than that were the families who had in good faith made their cash rent payments only to find out that their landlord had been foreclosed on. Because these families were undocumented with no Social Security number, we could not offer them "cash for keys" to assist them in finding another place to live.

Of course, this was amid Arizona's SB1070 legislative act (the 2010 Support Our Law Enforcement and Safe Neighborhoods Act, an anti-illegal immigration measure passed in the U.S.) that rocked our Hispanic communities. I am not sharing this to debate the subject or even to share my thoughts on SB1070, but for those of us in the trenches during that time, dealing with the real human beings faced with the foreclosure crisis—well, that part of our job sucked.

Even though that time was quite challenging, I still had one of my best years selling real estate and managed to get my name in the paper for selling the only $700,000-priced home in Peoria, Arizona.

While I watched the industry lose some amazing people, from escrow officers to lenders—the sky was literally falling—I was determined to have a different perspective. One of my favorite affirmations is "My perspective is my reality." A deeply rooted conviction to this belief caused me to create one of my best years in sales amidst the worst year ever recorded in the history of our industry.

After a while, I decided to take my knowledge and share it with my fellow agents by establishing a real estate school where I could develop and teach continuing education credit hours to Arizona REALTORS®. I wasn't interested in teaching pre-license classes. Instead, I focused on what I was passionate about.

The first class I wrote that was approved by the Department of Real Estate was a three-hour general credit class on DISC Personality Styles.

If you are reading this and don't know about DISC, it is a personality assessment tool that helps us understand our natural behavioral styles. I was able to share the content not only to help the agents understand how they tick but also how to use it when it came to successfully working with potential buyers and sellers.

Next, I wrote a class called the REO Jungle that helped agents understand the bank-owned contract process and how to effectively write offers that got accepted by the asset managers. I also worked closely with a couple of agents in the Phoenix market who were approved HUD home agents at the time. The HUD home class was approved by the Department of Real Estate as contract law credit hours.

Toward the end of the crash, and after negotiating more than 2,000 bank-owned contracts, I developed a two-day certification class that focused on selling government-owned homes—Freddie Mac and Fannie Mae—the offer process, the bank-owned contracts, inspections and repairs, escrow, and the closing process.

I assembled a panel of expert agents who had asset accounts with Freddie and Fannie in the Phoenix market to help me deliver the content. Unfortunately, as good as the twelve hours of continuing education material was, the market was changing, and I had missed the boat with my timing. It was an incredible experience, though, and I am so grateful for the handful of folks who saw my vision and supported me in creating it.

During this time, life coaching was becoming mainstream. If you know me, you know that I am always willing to share my two cents.

Well, one day, I was doing just that when the person on the other end of the conversation suggested that I should be a coach. I wish I could remember who it was that planted the seed for me because I'd like to thank them.

I now get to do what I love in this industry every day because that person put the idea out there. All these years later, I am still coaching (and selling real estate, too).

It is my sincerest goal in co-authoring this book with my mentor and dearest friend to be authentic, brutally honest, and share with you the reality of what it takes to be successful in any real estate market. I am truly blessed to have been a part of this industry since 1994, as it has provided me with a life that I never dreamed I could have.

Selling real estate, in my opinion, is the coolest job (next to being a rock star—although, when you do well, you do become a rock star in your own right). After years of trying to figure out what works and, more importantly, learning what doesn't, it is my goal to help you create a business that will make you a Rock Star REALTOR®. If you keep reading and apply the eight steps outlined in the following chapters, you will reach the rock star hall of fame in your business. So, keeping reading!

NATE ...

- 3 -
Arizona's Natural Resource Uses the Power of the Brand

Nobody in the world sells more real estate than RE/MAX.™

~ The truest real estate slogan in the entire world

When I left West USA in 1991, I was the number agent in the brokerage. The decision to move to RE/MAX was a pivotal point in my career. I started hanging out with like-minded people, RE/MAX agents who were hitting big numbers in transactions, and the agents I wanted to be like. I went from being the top guy at West USA to a speck at RE/MAX. It was a whole new playing field, which was both exciting and terrifying.

I have always been a fan of learning-based atmospheres; however, the opportunities that RE/MAX provided with training, support, and their events were mind-blowing – they brought the power of the brand.

After I made the move and got engrossed in this new company, my referral network started to grow. I had my CRS (Certified Residential Specialist) designation, but I hadn't gotten much referral business until I joined RE/MAX.

At the time (and I believe this is still true today), RE/MAX had the largest number of agents with their CRS designation. And they are pretty particular about keeping their business in the RE/MAX family. Because of this, my referral business blew up. Today, I continue to close plenty of referral business across the globe with RE/MAX agents who are in the CRS network.

*The CRS designation is difficult to obtain and getting it costs a bit of money. It is also not a designation for a person satisfied with being average. You have to have sixty transactions under your belt or $30 million in volume over the past five years.

I have attended every annual RE/MAX convention since 1991, and I made it my goal early on to use the opportunity to connect with as many agents as I could.

I'll write more about this topic in another chapter, but just know, at the time, I branded myself as "One of Arizona's Natural Resources." I have used this to promote my team and me over the last three decades, especially at the annual R4 Convention.

One year at the R4 Convention, the fun night entertainment was the Doobie Brothers. Knowing that, Sarah and I decided to purchase 2,500 sunglasses to hand out that night. On one arm of the glasses, it said, "One of Arizona's Natural Resources." The other arm said: www.nateshomes.com. It was awe-inspiring to look out over the crowd of REALTORS® from across the world and see 2,500 sunglasses dancing to the famous tunes of the Blues Brothers. Marketing ideas like that drove my referral business, and I can attribute a lot of my team's success to these sparks of inspiration, even all these years later.

I started in real estate in Phoenix, first at RE/MAX at the Pointe and then at the RE/MAX Integrity office located on Dunlap and the I-17.

The designated broker/owner happened to be the same gentleman, Ed McCloud, who I'd met when I answered an ad seeking real estate agents in the newspaper for *Better Homes and Gardens* in 1986. I didn't have the $300 to get my real estate license back then, so the brokerage paid for me to go to school.

After real estate school, I hung up my license with a small, no-frills local company, George Davis and Associates, and agreed to pay them a small monthly fee of about $25 plus a $100 transaction fee per closing. It's important to note that while I didn't end up working for *Better Homes and Gardens*, I did reimburse Ed the $300 he spent to send me to school.

As the city grew, so did the brokerage. Before long, Ed opened another office in Glendale, Arizona, off 67th Avenue and what was then called Beardsley Road (now the 101 Loop). This area was blowing up with new homes and commercial buildings, and one of the first master-planned communities—Arrowhead Ranch in the Valley of the Sun was in the process of being developed. The office was in the heart of the community, which was a smart investment by Ed and a game-changer for my team and business.

While I have a tremendous amount of respect and appreciation for Ed, unfortunately, back then, we did not share the same ideas surrounding service and support in the office.

I had a vision for more of a concierge-type experience for the agent and client. I soon learned if I was going to get that from a brokerage, I needed to hang my own shingle.

I just needed a place to do that.

One day, I was driving down Bell Road to a networking group I facilitated when I saw a sign with a rendering of a building at 71st Avenue and Bell Road in Glendale. After the meeting, I drove back by the lot, got out of my car, and walked around the construction site. I knew it was my spot where I wanted to open my real estate office.

I called our regional rep for RE/MAX and was told I couldn't get a franchise. Buying a RE/MAX franchise isn't as easy as raising your hand; guidelines and policies are in place to protect the quality of the brand and the broker/owners. But I didn't give up.

I called my longtime friend and RE/MAX colleague, Frank Russo, and told him I was going to buy a franchise. Then I asked him if he wanted to be my partner. (Truth be told, I was too scared to do it by myself anyway.)

I didn't know it until then, but Frank had also been kicking around the idea of leaving RE/MAX to open up Frank Russo Realty. He was already trying to purchase a piece of land at 83rd Avenue and Union Hills—so he was one step ahead of me in the plans.

Frank was leaving for a two-week trip to Istanbul, Turkey but told me he'd think about partnering with me and let me know if he was going to go for it when he got back from vacation. Ten days later, Frank called me from the airport in New York to tell me he was in.

On September 11, 2001, we held our first business meeting for the newly established franchise, RE/MAX Professionals. Yes, our very first day of business was held on the day the Twin Towers in New York were attacked, and our world was forever changed. What a day it was.

We'd had our first business meeting planned for weeks, the agenda written out, and even reserved the back room of Mimi's Café on Bell Road in Glendale, so we could provide breakfast for the new RE/MAX Professionals agents. I left the house really early that day, as I had a 6:00 am mastermind with my leads group (ironically, that was the last meeting we ever had) before I was to meet with Frank and the rest of the crew. I hadn't turned on the television that morning before I left the house, so I was clueless as to what was happening outside the restaurant.

As we were transitioning from one meeting to the next, I noticed one of the waitresses had tears in her eyes, so I asked her what was wrong. When she told me that a plane had hit the World Trade Center, I imagined a Cessna hitting the building and bouncing off.

At about a quarter of 9:00 am, our teams started to arrive at the restaurant. It was obvious that something was gravely wrong by the somber look on their faces; some had puffy, red eyes from crying. As each individual team member slowly filed into the restaurant; the air was filled with anticipation, sadness, freshly baked pastries, and strong black coffee.

Again, Frank and I had no idea that the Trade Centers had been attacked, so it was difficult for us to wrap our brains around what our people were feeling. We were filled with excitement and pride to be realizing our goal of opening a RE/MAX franchise, while this small group of agents who had taken a giant leap of faith to follow us into the unknown of being new franchise owners, sat in that restaurant stricken with fear and uncertainty. They questioned why we were there and what the future would look like.

It wasn't until I left the meeting and turned on the radio station KTAR in my SUV that I got an idea of how bad it really was. In the early afternoon, I watched the news coverage on the television—and that is when reality sunk in: the U.S. was under attack.

Upon reflection, should we have rescheduled the meeting? Maybe. But in the moment, we pressed forward because while we were all scared, we knew that we could not let it shake our determination and our commitment to the group of people who were now depending on us to show up and keep going no matter what. It was no longer about just Frank and me. We were owners of a real estate company, and these folks were depending on us to be their leaders through the eye of the storm.

Opening the brokerage was a roller coaster. It took a lot of work to build an office from the ground up. But building from scratch allowed us to leverage our vision. We could build the way we wanted to and create the environment and experience we wanted from the beginning. However, the timing of that building didn't go as planned. While Frank and I were at our first broker/owner training in Seattle, the official word got out that we were opening the franchise RE/MAX Professionals.

We had taken out an ad on the back page of the *Peoria and Glendale Recreation Guides*, which is a publication that at the time was delivered to every household in those two cities. The ad was bold and beautiful – it read: "Welcome to the future. RE/MAX Professionals opening September 2001."

Despite how great this ad looked, we didn't think through whether we should advertise our new business. Both the owner of our employing franchise and his managing broker lived in those two cities and thus, received a copy of the advertisement. It was no secret that Frank and I were opening a RE/MAX franchise, but the timing of the ad ruffled feathers so much that almost immediately, everyone licensed on my team, and Frank's was fired.

The next day, we managed to negotiate with Ed and his managing broker to keep our licenses at the brokerage. However, we had to work out of another location until our building was complete. Another critical part of this story is that we promised Ed we would never recruit any of his agents, and we never did. With the agreement in place, we could still sell real estate under the brokerage, but we had to empty our offices after hours in the dark through the back door.

For the next few weeks, while Frank, his team, my team, and I, and two independent agents waited for the building to be completed, my team worked out of my house with a cell phone set up as our dedicated line. It was passed like a hot potato from team member to team member. Sure, it was not ideal, but we made it work because our team was committed to the vision Frank, and I had.

All these years later, and I am extremely proud to share that many of those agents are still with us.

The word "gratitude" doesn't completely describe how I feel when I think about opening the franchise. It goes beyond gratitude. I have a deeply profound respect, appreciation, and pride for this group of agents who joined our new brokerage without a doubt that we would succeed. We would not be here today if it wasn't for their commitment, dedication, and unwavering faith in the vision. That is why they will forever be known as the "OGs" (original gangsters). Thank you to each of them.

A business partnership is like a marriage, and I consider myself very lucky to have had the partnership I did with Frank. We were like yin and yang, as I was the visionary and Frank was the realist. And while it was not always easy or profitable, we brought out the best qualities in each other. We continue to have a profound amount of respect for one another, and the level of trust we share is one of the key factors in our success.

If we didn't agree on something or one of us was adamant about a big decision, we trusted each other to make the right call for the business. I can say all these years later, and speaking from experience, if you don't have trust in a partnership, you have nothing.

There were only a few times over the past fifteen years that our partnership struggled. If we had to do it over again, I'd give this advice: make sure you have clear roles and responsibilities, so the expectation of each other is understood. We had no CEO in the beginning, and neither of us was the true leader. Sometimes that was because we didn't want to make the hard decisions that come with owning a real estate business.

When we let our egos get the best of us, it puts a strain on our relationships. In your partnership, if you start to think you are pulling more weight or have more responsibility, it's easy to think your shit don't stink. But because of the respect and trust we'd established early on, we learned from our mistakes. Regardless of our rare struggles, I'd pick Frank to be my business partner again and again.

> *"The road to success is always under construction."*
>
> *~ Lily Tomlin*

In 2001, at my very first broker-owner training at RE/MAX Headquarters in Denver, as a new franchise owner, I stood up and told everyone in the room that my goal was to have ten office locations in the Valley of the Sun and recruit 1,000 agents.

Well, we did just that … just not all at the same time. I got what I asked for, but I didn't have clarity on my ask. That's a great reminder to be clear about what you want because the universe is listening.

Shortly after our first location at 7111 W. Bell Road opened; I was in the city of Surprise when I passed by a little lake on the south side of Bell Road. Surprise was an up-and-coming area, blossoming with new, affordable homes and a growing commercial real estate presence. For some reason, I was drawn to this little lake. I called Frank and said, "I found our spot." We had barely opened our first location, so his response was something like, "What spot?"

RE/MAX ended up giving the Surprise location franchise to another broker/owner, which I was not happy about. But it didn't kill the vision I had in my mind's eye for an office location next door to that little lake.

A couple of years later, an employee who had been on my team for years, and was then a client care coordinator, took a call from a custom luxury home builder who wanted to break into commercial development. When I spoke to him, I told him of my vision for the office location at Surprise Fields—the location I was considering, and connected him with our commercial contact, Les. Of course, we didn't have any money to construct a commercial building, but he saw my vision and built out the office complex. We got first pick of the buildings, and about eighteen months later, our Surprise office location opened.

Because time had dragged a little between the time I had discovered Surprise and building our office there, Surprise was actually office number three.

Office number two came to be after I had gone for a ride on my motorcycle and come across an office complex in Avondale. It looked like the building owner was in trouble, and I thought if he was, maybe we could negotiate—and even buy the building with no money down. So, I called Frank and once again said, "I found our spot."

The Avondale office location opened pretty quickly. We owned both locations up until recently when Frank and I decided to take advantage of property values. We sold the Avondale location, and I replaced it with another building in the same complex.

Office locations four and five, the result of an acquisition deal we did with a local real estate brokerage, turned out to be a huge mistake and a decision driven by our out-of-proportioned egos.

One of the owners was Frank's fishing buddy, and this time, it was Frank who brought the deal to the table. Neither of the offices was in good retail locations, and to be honest, we didn't know what the hell we were doing when it came to office acquisitions. Eventually, we ended up closing both locations and only retained two of the agents who came with the acquisition.

The downtown Phoenix office location was number six, and while on paper the numbers made sense and the rent was cheap, we didn't have the revenue. Without a recruiter to put butts in the cubicles, it's hard to keep an office open. In fact, it's almost impossible to grow an office without a recruiter. To this day, recruiting is our Achilles' heel.

Before I share the story of offices 7-9, it's important to highlight that when the great crash started in 2006, we owned multiple office locations with approximately 300 agents.

During all this growth, there was a demand for quality property management to service the hundreds of investment properties we had sold to the folks from California. We opened a property management division that serviced 350 doors, and it was hugely successful and profitable – which saved our butts. Right before the crash, we sold that company, and the money we made off the sale funded RE/MAX Professionals. Without the decision to create a property management division and sell it at the perfect time in the market, we might have had to shut our doors.

> *"If a window of opportunity appears, don't pull down the shade."*
>
> *~ Tom Peters*

By now, you have heard the name Ed McCloud, and you know that he was instrumental in our decision to open RE/MAX Professionals. So, it was quite the feather in our cap when Ed presented us with the opportunity to acquire his franchise with ours. Remember part of the deal we made when we negotiated to keep our licenses in good standing until we could get our building finished? We kept our promise to him and never recruited any of his agents. In return, we were his first pick to buy his franchise which came with three amazing office locations.

I have always had respect for Ed as a businessman, as he is sly like a fox—but by now, we had figured out a thing or two about real estate acquisitions ourselves to make our partnership successful. The merger of RE/MAX Integrity with RE/MAX Professionals gave us office locations seven, eight, and nine.

By now, the market had begun to dramatically change, and we needed to pivot or be swept up by the crashing real estate market—and—so did our agents—especially—the ones we had acquired from the new merger. As a brokerage, we have always promoted education, whether that is attending our weekly classes, monthly meetings, or obtaining new designations.

The Certified Distressed Property Expert (CDPE) designation came about during the crash, and thankfully it saved a lot of agents and brokerages because it taught the industry how to navigate a "distressed" property sale.

Frank and I committed ourselves 100% with training, and as leaders, we jumped in with both feet to survive what was our "new normal."

Those who followed our leadership and changed their business model to adapt to selling distressed homes made it out alive, and those who didn't, well, I think you know what happened to them. That decision to jump on the CDPE designation saved our agents' careers as well as our clients' homes and their dignity.

In some of those lean years, Frank and I personally funded the business to help keep the doors open. While it was not profitable, I am extremely proud that we weathered the storm and lived to tell about it—not all broker-owners can say the same.

Office number ten was another acquisition, but this time it was a struggling RE/MAX franchise in Mesa, Arizona. Our corporate office is located in Glendale, and while I do believe it's possible to expand across the city, the geographic location was difficult to navigate without a solid management team in place. It didn't take very many instances of being stood up for recruiting appointments for me to realize it was a long hike to the East Valley. Again, this office location is another example of how important a good manager and/or recruiter is for a successful expansion.

The goal to own ten office locations didn't include a well-thought-out plan for keeping those offices open or funded. These locations may have happened because of my never-ending drive for more (and maybe a little ego). Today, the goal is to be lean, mean, and profitable while making a profound impact on the agents' lives who are a part of our amazing organization.

> ### "What counts is not necessarily the size of the dog in the fight. It's the size of the fight in the dog."
>
> ### ~ Dwight D. Eisenhower

Before the great crash, Frank and I had a lending partnership with Wells Fargo. We owned 49% of the business, which was hugely successful at the time. Up until this point, everything we did was a shared 50/50, but Frank saw what was coming in the market and jumped on the opportunity to apply for an REO account with Wells Fargo.

I was really struggling with the rapidly changing market and had massive resistance to working in the bank-owned arena. But one day, Frank had a hundred REO listings, while I barely had anything listed. This did not make me happy, but it lit a fire under my butt. I got to work applying for REO accounts.

My baby girl, Mila, was born just a few days before the RE/MAX convention that year, and while I had never missed one convention in my career with RE/MAX, the birth of my daughter was more important.

Still, her beautiful and incredibly supportive mother, Tonya, told me to go. I truly believe she knew more than me in that moment because the connections I made at R4 that year changed history for my team as well as my family and company.

The market was changing and quickly, and the brilliant leadership that comes from RE/MAX Headquarters has always been a beacon in the industry, providing education and opportunities for agents to pivot and adapt in changing market conditions. These two aspects of RE/MAX were about to work together very profitably.

That year at R4, Dave Liniger, the Founder of RE/MAX, brought in an REO presentation. After I watched it, I went to work doing what I do best—networking and connecting. Looking back now, I can see clearly that if I had not attended the convention that year, we would not be the company we are today. Thank you, Tonya.

At some point that same year, Sarah, and I attended a mastermind workshop in Chicago hosted by Coach Ken Goodfellow, and it was there that we mapped out the REO team plan. We knew we were going to need help to handle the sheer volume, but the volume was critical if we were going to be profitable.

We crunched the data down to the number of active listings we needed to hold at all times, figured how many days we had to turn them, the number of pending properties we required with a projected fall out rate, as well as the number of closings we had to do each month to be profitable. It was a mathematical machine, including successful accounts with Freddie Mac, Fannie Mae, Wells Fargo, and several other REO companies.

When a property goes to foreclosure, it gets assigned to an REO agent. But we were not prepared for the onslaught of new assignments we received when the account was activated. New assignments are new foreclosed property listings that we put onto the market after the property is secured.

We had to do a property check for occupants. If the property was occupied, we had to get them removed peacefully, if possible (meaning they hadn't trashed the place before they left), trash it out (because most of the time people left stuff behind, including pets—that was the worst!), then replace the locks and secure it if any windows were broken, etc.

After that, we had to put on the utilities if it was safe to do so. The utilities were in my name, and we were responsible for paying the monthly bills, as well as any repairs that we might have suggested on the property so we could sell it. Of course, the bank reimbursed us, but that was a tedious paperwork nightmare and took months to get the money back. If one step of their process was missed or done incorrectly, we were out the money. Period. At the peak, we were up to $100,000 in property expenses, and it was our bookkeeper's job to make sure we got all of it back. #NOPRESSURE

Once all of that was in place, we had to keep an eye on the place with weekly property checks and put it on MLS for sale—all the while reporting back to the asset manager who worked for the bank through their online portals. We had to take photos of everything to document the property condition as well because, at that time, people were breaking into vacant homes and stealing copper and AC units. Sometimes, they were even squatting in the properties because they were homeless. It was a shitshow!

I remember being in Florida at the NAR convention the day our Freddie Mac account switched on. In one day, we got thirty new assignments, and that first week, we received sixty assignments from all over the Valley, including as far as the farming community of Aguila, which is seventy miles from our office.

These foreclosure "assignments" would eventually become active listings we put on the market for sale after securing the property and working with the asset manager to establish a listing price.

It wasn't as easy at that, though. Within twenty-four hours of receiving the new assignment, we had to do a property check for occupants. Quite often, the squatters found living in the vacant properties were potentially dangerous for our field inspectors. We had to call the local police to assist plenty of times.

Like I noted, the goal was to peacefully remove them, so they didn't trash the home before they left. If we could do this, we could take advantage of what in the foreclosure world is called "cash for keys." For folks who didn't have any place to go or money to get there, the $1,000-2,500 cash incentive influenced them to leave without damaging or stripping the house. We have seen our share of plenty of homes gutted down to the wood studs and even concrete poured down sinks and toilets.

Once we had possession of the home, we worked with local vendors to prepare it for sale and make sure the home was safe enough for the public to tour the property. Rarely were any repairs made to bank-owned properties, so we dealt in "buyer beware" and "as-is" purchases.

Because we had hundreds of REO assignments across the Valley of the Sun, we had three full-time field inspectors. Their only responsibility was to drive around the city doing weekly checks on our assignments to make sure they were secure.

They were required to document the condition of the property with date and time stamped photography of things like A/C units, evidence of the water being on, and other general conditions, which were reported back to the asset managers. During those financially dark years in our economy, people were breaking into vacant homes to steal copper piping, air conditioning units, and anything else that had value on Craigslist. It wasn't uncommon for a field inspector to find a homeless person who had moved into a property or an overly excited buyer who had somehow gotten the combination to the lockbox.

Two Hellish REO Transactions

The first property that I will never forget was about a week out from closing. The buyer had loan docs signed, and their down payment money was at the title company. We were literally ready to close when Sarah got an email from the asset manager instructing her to cancel the escrow because the assignment was being pulled back by the REO company.

It turned out that the previous owner was contesting the foreclosure proceedings, and the REO company could not move forward selling it until the issue was resolved. Fine print in their contracts allowed for a property to be taken back or, in other contracts, to be taken off the market. In this case, the buyer had somehow gotten the combination code for the lockbox. When we did a property check, we discovered they'd had the entire interior of the home painted—to a tune of $5,000 out of their pocket. In anticipation of closing in a week, they just wanted it to be freshly painted before moving in. *Yikes!* Let's just say they were not very happy.

The second story dealt with another property about to close escrow. In fact, it did close late on a Friday afternoon, but the title company failed to inform the buyer, the buyer's agent, or us—the listing agent. Our field inspector was there mid-day on Friday to do a property check, and all was safe and sound. Well, sometime between the property check and Monday morning, we found out the home had been recorded into the new buyer's name, and the property had been broken into and gutted. In that case, the REO company did do the right thing and made the repairs to the home. The buyer in that situation was happy because he'd bought a newly renovated property for a steal of a price.

We sold REOs in all shapes, sizes, and locations, even $15,000 homes with a view of the Palo Verde Nuclear Plant! In our best REO year, we closed 679 properties, with the majority of them being bank-owned. While it was a bloody slaughterhouse on the economy, we'd like to think we made a difference in our community by being the "friendly REO team." It is because we fought through the storm that my team and company are still standing.

Our mission is to have a profound impact on agents' lives.

In the beginning, Frank and I thought we could recruit like-minded agents to work for our brokerage, but as it turns out, we aren't just a place to hang a real estate license; we are a company that changes agents' lives through our training, support, and leadership, and that leadership starts at the top in the RE/MAX Headquarters. Being a part of this outstanding organization has shaped my life and ultimately allowed me to leave behind a legacy I never dreamed possible as a young boy growing up in the hood.

I am beyond blessed with a beautiful family, a gorgeous home, and nice cars to drive, but as great as all that is, it's not enough.

I feel an obligation—maybe a better word is passion—about giving back to my community and to the industry that has afforded me this amazing life. I want to develop and help agents live their best lives, just like my mentors have helped me do.

Having a profound impact on someone's life is about so much more than how much money they make or how many trophies they collect. It's a quality of life. It's an experience. It's an opportunity. This is not a responsibility I take lightly. There are still plenty of sleepless nights because the people in my life are so important to me, and I want to make sure they are happy and fulfilled. It's hard to let go and relax when so much is at stake.

> *"The task of the leader is to get his people from where they are to where they have not been."*
>
> *~ Henry Kissinger*

Being a part of the RE/MAX organization has changed my life.

From day one, joining the RE/MAX organization has opened my eyes to goals and ideas that I would never have been exposed to. Great leadership helps you think bigger, and it offers support. Support paves the way for innovation and inspiration. Great leadership creates a winning experience for the agents, the brokerage, and ultimately the consumer.

The RE/MAX brand equals opportunity. I hope that when agents think about RE/MAX Professionals, they feel the same way.

I also hope that as you continue reading this book, you see how the power of the brand has contributed to our successes. Regardless of if you are a RE/MAX agent or not, I would encourage you to align with a brokerage that provides the level of support, education, and resources you need to dominate any real estate market. Who you hang your license with matters for your business' success.

Three+ decades, and it's been a great ride. I wouldn't have been able to write this book if it hadn't been for the power of the brand. Thank you, RE/MAX, and thank you, RE/MAX Professionals.

Your B.H.A.G. Blueprint

- 4 -
What's Your Blue Dot?

"People assume everyone wants to reach their potential and be the best they can be. I've concluded that most only want to be average and just do enough to get by."

~ Nick Saban, Six-time Championship Football Coach, University of Alabama

Nate and I have a favorite acronym for goal planning: B.H.A.G., which stands for Big, Hairy, Audacious Goals.

Yes, you want to have a goal that is worth striving for, a goal that makes you want to jump out of bed each morning because you can't wait to get to work. But a goal should not be so easy that you could do it tomorrow and take the rest of the year off. You also don't want to set a goal that does not inspire you or is so ridiculous that you feel intimidated by it.

A B.H.A.G. is somewhere in between making our palms a little sweaty, our stomach a bit queasy, and it causes our hearts to beat with excitement.

If you read the quote above, and your face felt a little flush with irritation, then it hit a nerve worth exploring.

The intent of the B.H.A.G. is to make you uncomfortable, so you'll think a little deeper.

Ask yourself if you are living up to your potential.

By nature, most salespeople are competitive, so the idea that you might be "average" will create discomfort. Keep in mind that average is not bad if that is your goal. We're guessing that's not the case since you are reading this book. Chances are, you are looking for more in your life and your real estate career.

Here's an analogy you can relate to when it comes to assessing your progress. All professional football teams and high school teams review their games on video to see where they can improve. As real estate agents, we just go through our day without taking a moment to figure out where we are lacking. Five years later, when you come up for air, you are divorced, broke, and owe the IRS for unpaid taxes (and you might not have the money to pay the bill). *But wait, what happened? I am selling real estate, and I have the trophies in my garage to prove it!*

Can you relate?

In April of 2021, there were more than 62,000 licensed agents in Maricopa County (Phoenix Metro area). Nationally, there are nearly 1.5 million active agents, according to the National Association of REALTORS® (NAR).[1] Sadly, NAR also reports that 87% of agents are out of the business within five years.

Many agents struggle to sell enough homes per year to pay their bills, and when we break it down, some of them are living below the poverty line. That is because most agents are not thinking of their real estate practice as a business. Those who dominate the real estate market think like entrepreneurs, not 1099 contractors.

The first order of business is to *stay in business*, which involves knowing who you are and what you want.

We have provided these steps to help you get there.

Step One: Define your Vision

When I ask agents why they got into real estate, my favorite responses are: "I like people," "I like looking at houses," or "For the flexibility." This is the biggest "F" word in the real estate industry (there is no flexibility on a Saturday morning when a demanding buyer wants to see a house)!

Let's be honest. Real estate is a wealthy business, and most of us want to earn more money to support our big "why" in life—which takes us back to 1986 when Nate was newly licensed in real estate.

---

1 *"Quick Real Estate Statistics."* **Research and Statistics**, *National Association of REALTORS®, November 11, 2020. https://www.nar.realtor/research-and-statistics/quick-real-estate-statistics.*

In Nate's Words ...

The year prior, I'd met a gentleman named Cam, who was dating my sister-in-law, and he happened to be a REALTOR®. He rolled up to the house in a 280Z Datsun car, wearing ostrich-skinned boots, a matching belt, and Jordache jeans. I asked him what he did for a living, and he said, "I sell real estate."

I bugged him to tell me more, but in truth, I just wanted to know how much money could be made selling real estate.

He went on to tell me that he had made $86,000 that year, and it was only August! At that time, I was a concrete laborer working 60+ hours a week and making around $40,000 a year. Contrast that with the well-dressed gentleman, driving an expensive car, and dating a good-looking lady—it was all working for him.

At that moment, I thought to myself, *I want to be a REALTOR®.*

The very next day after meeting Cam, I picked up the newspaper, and that's when I saw the ad from **Better Homes and Gardens** and signed up to get my real estate license.

At that time, the three of us: my wife, Brandi, and I were living paycheck to paycheck, and I thought if I could just sell one or two houses a year, it would give me a little extra cash to buy the things I wanted, like a big-screen TV or a trip to Disneyland with my family.

That is how I started in real estate, but thirty-five years ago, I didn't know it was going to turn into my career. I just jumped in with no training or plan other than my shallower aspirations. However, I was willing to work for what I wanted once I saw the opportunities available to me.

After I got my real estate license, I quickly realized I had created an opportunity for my family and me that was the real deal, but I still had no clue what I was doing.

I knew I had to invest in my education through designations. One of them was the Certified Residential Specialist (CRS) I told you about earlier. Three years into my career, I went to the first-ever CRS Celebration event in Las Vegas, Nevada.

When I got there, I noticed some of the agents had a blue dot on their name badge, and they were making a pretty big deal over them. I soon discovered that those agents with the blue dot had sold over 100 homes in the last twelve months. They were also the speakers on stage—the agents that everyone oohed and ahhed over.

I had never met someone who had sold that many homes, nor did it ever occur to me that an agent could! That was my Roger Bannister moment (the first person to break a four-minute mile). I could see those top producing agents on the stage like Ralph Roberts and Phyllis Laborski. They were just like me; they put their pants on the same way. My mind was blown and seeing and hearing them was all it took. Once I realized that volume could be achieved, I knew I would make it to that level in my career.

> ***I made it my mission to get a blue dot at the next CRS Celebration. That was my business plan—the blue dot.***

The blue dot signified so much more than just selling a bunch of houses as a solo agent. It was the recognition that I never got as a kid growing up. It was the confirmation I desperately needed that I was good enough. It meant that I finally belonged among my peers. The blue dot agents made up a special tribe signifying a level of success I'd never imagined possible. The drive to be a part of that group challenged me to tap into my innovation and changed the course of decades of my life.

I went to the second annual CRS Celebration expecting to get my blue dot. After I'd received my envelope with my name badge, I checked it twice—but there was no blue dot. *I made the sales, but where is my blue dot*, was all I could think.

I asked the lady who checked me in, "Where's my blue dot?!?" To my dismay, I was informed that they had decided not to do the blue dot. *But I sold over a hundred homes—all I want is my blue dot!*

Although I was devastated with no blue dot to my name at the year-two CRS Celebration, the moral of the story is to surround yourself with agents who sell more houses than you. You don't have to be seven years into your career to have your Roger Bannister moment—you can have it today.

Dare to consider the possibilities and create a plan to support your vision. I never had a plan in writing; the blue dot was my plan. I did, however, have a very clear and precise vision in my head. Upon reflection, I know I could have built my business and career in a much smarter way if I had known better and if I had a plan in writing to support my vision.

> *"If you don't design your own life plan, chances are you'll fall into someone else's plan. And guess what they have planned for you? Not much."*
>
> *~ Jim Rohn*

At the start of the year, agents will ramp up prospecting daily and building up their listing inventory. (January is a very busy listing month in most markets.) Then they'll get too busy servicing the clients they have under contract and will stop prospecting because they have no time. Once the deals close, they'll run out of leads and start prospecting again. It is very typical to see peaks and valleys in an agent's production between spring and summer and again in the fall and winter.

Most agents don't know to create systems and processes that support their businesses, like defining a Top 50 client list, having a CRM, or outlining follow-up plans. (We will go into more details about these elements later in the book.)

An effective rule of thumb to use is that if you do something more than three times in your business, it needs a documented process. Most agents are sporadic and reactive because they do not create efficiency in their daily activities. Seventy-five percent of a real estate transaction concerns non-dollar productive activities, yet the average agent will refuse to delegate because they don't want to spend money on an assistant, or they believe they are the only one capable of completing certain tasks.

Taking this action involves a mindset shift …

But how do you move from 1099 behavior to thinking like an entrepreneur?

It starts with getting crystal clear on what it is you want and how badly you want it. Are you willing to suffer for it? *Are you passionate about it? Are you willing to do what it takes to make it happen, no matter what?*

If the answer is "yes," then you are on the right track.

A successful real estate career business plan looks something like this:

My life aspirations are (fill in the blanks):

- I need to make [insert how much you need] money to fund it.
- I need to sell [insert number] to make the money.
- The functions and responsibilities of my business are [fill in the blank].
- The strategies and activities I must do daily for my business to succeed are [fill in the blank].
- I need to learn [fill in the blank].
- I need to track [fill in the blank].
- My ROI (Return On Investment) is [insert number].

Most people only live up to 25% of their potential. That is a lot of houses and commissions left on the table for your competition to grab.

> *"Money won't create success, the freedom to make it will."*
>
> *~ Nelson Mandela*

Not very many of us are motivated by the idea of making more money; we are, however, driven by the way we feel when we accomplish something we set out to do.

If you grew up poor and you want to make enough money to send your kids to college, that is a clearly defined goal but how you feel about sending your child is your motivation. When you imagine their life as a thriving adult with a great career and a beautiful family—the feelings of pride and joy become the motivation to get out of bed in the morning.

When a deal is about to fall apart, or you've missed dinner again for the third time this week (and trust us, it will happen if you stay in the business long enough!), ask yourself how connected you are to the vision or goal. Your unwavering belief in the outcome will give you the motivation and perseverance to not only survive but dominate any real estate market.

Recap Step One – Define Your Vision: What's Your Blue Dot? Get Clear on Your "Why" and How to Make It Happen.

Gaining Clarity on Your "Why"

In addition to writing this book, we have created a real estate journal to support the eight concepts we are teaching you, titled *Your Real Estate Journey to Abundance: 8-Step Journal.* In the journal, you will find space to write down what your aspirations look like in the eight key areas of life: **Lifestyle, Household, Relationships, Faith, Fitness, Friends, Community, Career, and Finance**. You can use it as a companion guide to this book and order it here: REM.AX/YOURREALESTATEJOURNEYTOABUNDANCE. When you are journaling, please don't rush to fill it out just for the sake of doing it. Instead, be intentional. If now is not the right time to work on your "why," then come back to it when you can give yourself the time you need. Your "why" in life deserves an intentional, focused effort.

But before you dedicate time to journaling, let's take a look at the Wheel of Life.

THE WHEEL OF LIFE

The Wheel of Life centers on the eight key areas we tend to spend most of our time and energy developing. And just like a wheel on a car, these areas move us forward in business and life.

The catch is that most of us don't have a perfectly round wheel. That can make successfully navigating the world a bit of a challenge.

To get the most out of the Wheel of Life, visit HTTPS://REM.AX/WHEEL to claim your own wheel. Then highlight or shade in the percentage that you feel is most accurate for your life currently in each of the eight areas.

Next, highlight or shade in the percentage where you want to see improvement or change in the next twelve months.

As you begin to write your business plan in the following pages, consider how those goals and dreams shape your Wheel of Life. Be strategic in using your goals to make improvements or changes so that your life will become more and more round as you move throughout the next year.

What does your wheel of life look like currently?

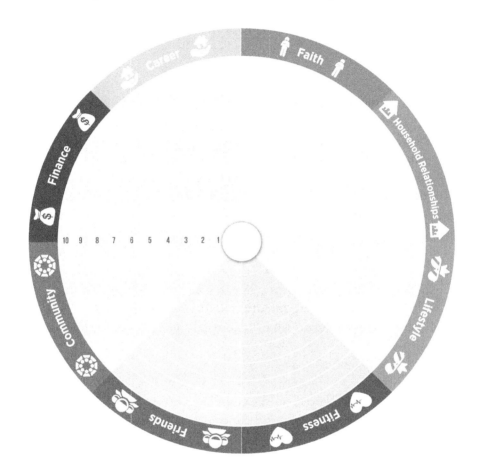

How do you want your wheel of life to look?

Now let's get down and dirty! Download a free B.H.A.G. blueprint at REM.AX/BHAGBLUEPRINT to help you identify specific goals you want to accomplish in all seven areas over the next twelve months. Then identify what might be an impediment to stop you from getting there. Be honest. There are no wrong or right answers.

Want to up your accountability? Join our private Facebook group, *8 Ways to Dominate Any Real Estate Market*. Just head over to Facebook and look us up, then take a photo of your "why" and post it in the group!

- 5 -
The Three Most Dreaded Words

"Many people are in the dark when it comes to money, and I'm going to turn on the lights."

~ Suze Orman

In 1990, Nate joined RE/MAX, and in 1991, he went to his first RE/MAX convention. It was at that event that Nate decided he would be the number one RE/MAX agent in the region—the territory between Arizona, Nevada, and New Mexico.

As Nate says, "That was my B.H.A.G."

☙

In Nate's Words ...

Becoming the number one agent had a pretty steep price tag. Sure, I had the plaques and the recognition from my peers, RE/MAX, and the industry, but it wasn't a well-designed plan. It cost me my marriage, my relationship with my children, and I owed the IRS over $100,000 in taxes. In the early 90s, that was a lot of money, especially when I was selling $50,000 houses. (It's a lot of money today, too.)

I was so driven in business, but I let everything else fall apart.

I didn't have a plan or a budget, just an insatiable drive for the number one spot. I achieved the goal, but it cost me everything. I also took my team and my other relationships for granted, and I will admit in those days, I had a short fuse. Team members could tell you stories of me threatening to cut off a finger if someone got a phone number wrong. I was so obsessed with being the number one RE/MAX agent that I lost sight of life.

On the surface, I was the man, or at least in my mind, I thought I was the shit, but I was not thinking right.

I remember being at a RE/MAX awards event when we had been crowned the number one team in the region. I was about to walk across the stage to receive the RE/MAX Eagle Award, and my now ex-wife was crying at the table. Everyone thought it was so touching that she was crying (they assumed she was crying tears of joy for my achievement). However, she was crying because she was a broken-hearted woman. I am not proud of those days. But I share this with you because it is my hope that you can learn from my mistakes.

A successful career in real estate doesn't have to cost you everything if you have a plan. That is the goal of this book—to share our story (the good and bad), so you can have a solid, tried-and-true plan to get you the results you want out of your real estate business and, most importantly—the results you want for your life.

On a funny note …

Over the years, as we consistently ranked as the number one team in the RE/MAX region, I accumulated quite a few of those plaques, which eventually ended up in my garage, stacked along the walls.

During a trip to Chicago for a RE/MAX Broker/Owner event, unfortunately, my home was broken into. We think it was someone who knew me or at least my vehicle because the only thing the thieves went after were the shiny rims on my Escalade. They were twenty-four-inch wheels, which were the baddest (and most expensive) rims on the market at the time. Instead of leaving my SUV on the floor in my garage, after stripping my rims, they used the plaques to jack up the vehicle. It was quite the scene to behold, and although it was not cool to have my home burglarized, my team and I still get a pretty good laugh out of the story even years later.

> **A budget is telling your money where to go instead of wondering where it went."**
>
> **~ Dave Ramsey**

༺༻

Sarah Speaks …

I joined RE/MAX in 1997 as a buyer's agent on Nate's Team. When I went to my first awards event that spring, like Nate, I had a similar experience as his blue dot revelation at the CRS Celebration. When I saw all the other agents receive their plaques, I couldn't wait to come back the next year and walk across the stage to get *my* plaque.

In my first year on the team, I outproduced Nate's veteran buyer's agent, which was a pretty big accomplishment considering his experience and stature on the team. I loved real estate so much and had such a drive to succeed that most days, I was the first person in the office and the last to leave.

A few years into my career, I was making more money than I could ever imagine possible. But like Nate, I did not have a plan or budget—I did, however, have some nice jewelry and some overdue taxes! In just three short years, I found myself owing the IRS $50,000—a debt that I did not have the money for.

Whether you are new to the business or a seasoned veteran wondering if the IRS will levy your bank account, please *take* our advice in this chapter. Handle your business with them, and don't let it get out of control.

જી

Step Two: Your Business Plan and Working Budget.

That is why we have to talk about these three most dreaded words:

"Business Plan" and "Budget"

A written business plan and budget are a must if you want to survive in any industry as an entrepreneur. None of us like the word budget because it reminds us of sixth grade "homework." So, we like to call it a "spending plan," which leaves room to have some fun while building your real estate legacy.

We have talked about the importance of knowing how many homes you need to sell to fund your extraordinary life. Let's take a deeper look at that.

Let's say you want to make $250,000 next year, and the average sales price in your area is $300,000. This is the math for this example:

$$\begin{array}{r} \$300,000 \\ \times \quad 3\% \text{ commission} \\ \hline \$9,000 \text{ paycheck} \end{array}$$

$250,000 divided by $9,000 gives us approximately 28 units that we must sell to hit the income goal.*

*This calculation does not take into account office splits, team splits, taxes, and other business expenses you need to build into your budget, which changes your transactional benchmark. Commission rates are not standard across all markets, and this is only an example of how to calculate the basic math.

Next, please take a few minutes to jot down your desired income goals in the space provided below.

Your Economic Requirement

First, identify your Desired Gross Income, then add your Budgeted Expenses (including taxes, office splits, and expenses). Next, you will need to know your Average Commission Rate and Your Average Sales Price.*

*If you are new to the industry, use the averages for your office or market.

Transaction Benchmark Requirements

1)   Desired Gross Income: $ _____

\+   Budgeted Expenses: $ _____

=   Total Revenue Needed: $ _____

2) Your Average Sales Price: $ _____

× Average Commission Rate: % _____

= Average Commission Check: $ _____

3) Total Revenue Needed: $ _____

÷ Average Commission Check: $ _____

= Total Units Needed: # _____

The number of homes you need to sell to hit your Gross Commission Income (GCI) goal is your transactional benchmark; you should know this number and where you are each month in accordance to your unit or income goal by heart. It's far more effective planning to know the desired outcome then track it to make sure you are on target, weekly, monthly, and quarterly.

If you want to get micro-granular with your goal, study the peak selling months in your business and market. You may find that you sell more homes in the spring or summer than you do in the winter months. Instead of focusing on making the same number of sales each month, consider adjusting your monthly unit goals to meet those peak selling times.

EXAMPLES:

January:	1	unit
February:	2	units
March:	3	units
April:	3	units
May:	4	units
June:	5	units
July:	5	units
August:	4	units
September:	3	units
October:	3	units
November:	2	units
December:	2	units

At the very least, you should know your weekly, monthly, and quarterly unit goals to hit your desired GCI. Remember that everything you do (or don't do) today doesn't impact your business today—it impacts your business the next 45-60 days from now.

> *"I worked for a menial's hire, only to learn, dismayed, that any wage I had asked of life, life would have paid."*
>
> *~ Unknown*

With just a little bit of effort, most agents could sell twelve houses in a year. A good aim is to sell one house a week and then take four weeks off! Real estate is a very simple business if you work it right.

Your business plan needs to include a complete 12-month marketing plan (which we cover in Chapter 8), the number of homes you need to sell to fund your lifestyle, and your budget. The budget needs to be fully comprehensive, meaning that you will include all expenses as they relate to your business, down to the money you spend at Starbucks on your way to the office every day, the college tuitions that need to be saved, the retirement home you dream about, the new car you want to buy and so on.

The grand total number is going to scare you. It is meant to.

Most Americans live paycheck to paycheck and would be bankrupt in thirty days of a crisis. The reality is even worse for the typical real estate agent. If you want to dominate the real estate market, a budget is a vital, non-negotiable component of a successful business blueprint. There is no excuse not to have one.

Create the time to do it, keep it updated, and be honest about your spending habits. If you don't know the rate of return (ROI) of something you are paying for, then figure it out. If it is not paying you back, kill it.

> *The definition of insanity is doing the same thing over and over and expecting different results.*
>
> *~ Albert Einstein*

Whatever you spend money or time on, you need to know the ROI. A good rule of thumb is to have a return of 3-4 times the money spent. If it is not in the budget, then don't spend money on it unless you can afford to. The goal is to be profitable at the end of the year, meaning that you have paid all your bills, AND you still have money left over.

Here's a more exact look at ROI and lead generation.

If you spent $60,000 a year on big online lead gen, and you made $120,000 GCI, you made your money back, but it wasn't truly profitable when you take into consideration the hours spent to convert and sell the leads, the wear and tear on your car, taxes, office splits, and other costs spent to get the deal closed. Not to mention the time away from other money-making activities. Taking into account those calculations, you end up netting closer to $30,000 at the end of the year.

If you are a team leader, the ROI is even less after you calculate the splits with your buyer agents. You might ask yourself *would it be better not to buy leads or to buy leads and make no profit?*

It's critical that you know the costs of paying for leads, that you can calculate the return on investment, and that you are smart when it comes to how you spend money to generate new business.

Another cost that most agents don't truly understand is direct mail farming. If you are considering a farm area, you need to budget at least twelve months of marketing expenses, with the expectation that you will not see a dime in return for a minimum of six months. Too many agents start and then give up because they can't afford longevity in their marketing endeavors, which is a giant waste of money and resources.

Let's take this a step further.

Assume you are farming a community of 1,000 homes with a turnover rate of 7% (rule of thumb is a community where 5-7% of those homes sell annually). That would give you a target of seventy homes that will potentially sell in the next year. Meaning out of 1,000 homes, only seventy people will be thinking about moving, and the other 930 won't do anything. Even more importantly, only about 1% or seven people per month will be thinking about selling when they get your piece in the mail.

Let's descend another level in this analysis.

We have a target of seventy homes. Now, let's say there are five agents who live there working the community and who have 60% of the market share or forty-two listings closed. That leaves 40% or twenty-eight listings for the rest of the agents in that community, who might be farming the area, too. *Would three sales a year from your farm be considered successful? Let's do the math.*

If you only got 10% of those listings, you'd have an ROI of approximately $27,000 at an average paycheck of $9,000 (3 x $9,000 = $27,000).

Farming is a high numbers game, but if you understand the numbers and analyze the data and costs related to marketing, it can be profitable. If you spent $1,000 a month for six months, and the listing price point is $300,000, you could make your money back—plus get your name out there as a community expert. If you have a listing and marketing plan like what Workman Success Systems teaches, you could expect another 1.5 buy-side transactions for every listing you put on the market.

You must be crystal clear about the budget for direct mail and understand the numbers before you *ever* invest in marketing. Too many agents are looking for a fast return, and farming takes watering the crop over time.

We'll wrap up this chapter by giving you two real examples that recently happened to Nate on a direct mailer. Two pieces went out to 5,000 homes at a cost of approximately $2,000 per piece. Out of 5,000 postcards, two people raised their hands to list their homes. Both of those properties equaled a net $12,000 commission.

Here's the math:

	$12,000	Commission
x	2	Listings
	$24,000	GCI
−	$4000	Marketing Costs
	$20,000	Net Profit

$4000 x 4 times ROI = $16,000 (this piece actually had a 5 x ROI).

> ### *"Stop setting goals. Goals are pure fantasy unless you have a specific plan to achieve them."*
>
> ### *~ Stephen Covey*

In the example above, we used an annual income goal of $250,000. However, your goal should be specific to your lifestyle and expenses. At the end of your budget spreadsheet, if your grand total doesn't match your annual income goal, you will need to adjust your transactional goal until there is enough money to cover your expenses.

Once you have this number and do the math on how many houses that means you have to sell, put this goal up somewhere in your office, home, bathroom, or on your cell phone screen saver, etc. (Preferably, place it on all of them) so that you can see it every single day.

The more you hang out with your goals, the more likely you are to hit the target. It won't do you any good to write a business plan and stick it in a drawer somewhere in your office (or the trunk of your car) and use the hope-and-pray strategy.

Be intentional.
Be proactive.

Create a dream board or an affirmation that you hang on the wall or on a mirror you pass by throughout the day.

Your business plan needs to become a part of your DNA; it needs to be a part of your daily routine, meaning the budget needs to be kept up to date with honest reporting.

You can find plenty of options for creating a budget online, as well as in various books. We have also provided a link at the end of this chapter so that you can download the budget we use for free. Don't stick your head in the sand because you dread the word "budget," or you don't know how to create a business plan.

Ask for help if you don't know where to start. Take control of your money and leverage it to build a lifetime of wealth and happiness.

Recap Step Two: Create a Business Plan and Working Budget.

While writing this book, we designed a budget specific for REALTORS®, and you can download a free copy at REM.AX/REALTORBUDGET.

- 6 -
Our Magic Pill

"Intentions compressed into words enfold magical power."

~ Deepak Chopra

The concept of a "perfect week" is not new; in fact, we have been talking about it for many years as an industry. Most of us have heard that we need to plan our "big rocks." A big rock is a first priority, like date night with your significant other, going to church, having dinner with your kids, hitting the gym for a workout, etc.

No one talks about how freaking hard it is to live by a schedule in real estate while navigating active buyers, demanding sellers, multiple offers, contingency deadlines, the competition, and so on.

And no one has addressed the mental impossibility that comes up just from using the word "perfect." (Is there really such a thing as perfect?).

Sarah grew up with a narcissistic mother; no matter how hard she tried, whatever she did, was never good enough for her. And as a recovering control freak with a high "D" personality (read on for an in-depth definition of what the DISC assessment is), the very idea of perfectionism is enough to make her want to pull out her eyebrows, one by one!

Let's unpack this a little more and turn this concept into a magic pill for both your life and business.

Welcome to the DISC Personality Assessment

Nate first learned about DISC from his days as a "star" with the real estate organization, Star Power and when anyone joined his team, one of the first things they had to do was take a DISC assessment. Sarah was fascinated by the DISC assessment from day one, and over the years, she has studied a variety of personality assessment tools on the market, but she's always returned to the ease and accuracy of DISC. She was so passionate about how it impacted her life and her communication skills that she wrote an accredited real estate renewal class on the topic that she taught for four years because she wanted her fellow agents and the industry to know more about how to utilize it in their business and life. Today, she continues to teach about the DISC assessment without the continuing ed credit.

Nate and Sarah have a few invaluable stories about how DISC has helped people become better team leaders and agents.

At the time of one listing appointment with a lovely family that had two young children, Nate was the proud owner of a custom Jim Nasi motorcycle. This quickly became the topic of discussion with the husband, who had a shared love of feeling the wind in your hair as you cruise down the open road on the back of a sexy black hunk of hotrod metal. This should have been Nate's first clue that the husband was a strong "I" personality—as is he. It was an immediate and effortless connection in their personalities. ("I" personalities are drawn to each other like a moth to a lightbulb.)

As the conversation went on, Nate thought he had a great connection and had nailed the listing appointment, only to later find out that they had listed their home with another agent. Upon reflection, this is what we would learn from that appointment. As Nate and the husband were metaphorically planning a cross-state adventure on their motorcycles, the wife was envisioning how she would tell her two beautiful young children that their father had suffered an untimely and irresponsible death. *Who would she invite to his funeral, and goodness, what should she wear?*

She was a high "S" personality, which is the caretaker, nurturing momma-bear. And Nate was coming across as a threat to her family—the one thing you never want to do when dealing with a strong "S" personality. There was no way Nate was listing their house because there was no way her husband was *ever* getting a motorcycle. Lesson: pay attention to clues. People naturally leak who they are, and human beings have a deeply rooted need to be seen, heard, and connected to. Nate did a great job of connecting with the husband, but he failed to meet and protect the needs of the momma "S."

Next, Sarah shares an embarrassing but important story about herself. She had to cover for Nate on a listing appointment and literally grabbed the file on the fly so she would not be late. She walked into the gentleman's house like a storm of frazzle and ditz raining in unpreparedness. She remembers saying to the man that she hadn't had time to look at the comps. In retrospect, she should have just walked out then since there was no way she was landing the appointment. She wouldn't have gotten the listing even if she'd had some superpowers to magically make the Taj Mahal appear.

She later realized the seller was a high "C" personality and her lack of preparedness was completely unacceptable to him. How could he trust anything she was saying or believe that she was an expert when she didn't even have time to review the data on his home? "C's" are dangerously accurate. (They can do math in their head like a wizard!) Their trust is earned, not given at free will. Lesson: be factual; be accurate, and reschedule if there isn't enough time to be overly prepared when dealing with a "C."

This last story has to do with using the DISC personality tool for hiring. This experience cemented Sarah's belief in the importance of using DISC in business, especially when it came to running Nate's team.

*

When we were hiring for a listing manager, we met this beautiful, spunky, outgoing blonde bombshell of a lady who could have appeared on the cover of a glamor magazine. We were in love at first sight! She had been referred to us by a friend who happened to be an agent in our office. Instead of having a formal interview with her, we decided to go to happy hour to get to know each other and brought along her friend, who happened to be the life of any party. Clue number one: "I" personalities *love* a good party.

Both of us are high "I/D" personalities, so it is easy for us to get distracted by the shiny object, and *she* was the shiny object with her experience in property management. (At the time, Nate owned several rental properties.) Besides her experience in rentals and the fact she had her real estate license, this gal was not a good fit for the job. However, we got caught up in the "fun." Her salary package was negotiated on a cocktail napkin later that evening. Fast forward a few weeks into her employment when Sarah noticed behavior that is to this day still etched in her memory banks.

"I" personalities by nature are not organized people (sorry "I's" reading this! The struggle is real, though), and they lack the ability to tell time, meaning they will get caught up in whatever is fun and appealing in the moment. They don't like timelines or boring details because, after all, they are the life of the party and who wants to bring a lame spreadsheet to the party? This new employee's high "I" traits were almost off the charts. So, the idea that we put her into a desk job that required running comps, entering listings in the MLS, and pulling reports was setting her up for failure before she cashed her first paycheck.

Sarah noticed during the day—and this is no exaggeration—that she would sit at her desk for thirty minutes tops before she had to get up and walk around. She would wander the office hallways, looking for any signs of life that she could talk to, get a fresh cup of coffee, or chat up the front desk staff. All day, she would do this. Until one day, she got fired for messing up on a "detail" that cost us a listing. We failed her by not paying attention to her natural gifts and abilities as a human being. She was never going to be a data person, no matter how much we liked her. She was never going to thrive in a role that felt more like a ball and chain that kept her bound to a desk in front of a computer screen.

⁂

To this day, when Sarah coaches or teaches about using DISC to hire a team member, she is adamant that DISC should be employed to attract and hire the right personality style for the job, whether that is a client care coordinator, a bookkeeper, buyer's agent, listing partner or marketing person. When you bring someone on to your team or into your business, they become more than just an employee. They become a part of your life and your family. They depend on you for their livelihood. It is critical that we don't take that lightly because it's a huge responsibility. The DISC tool helps us quickly determine what a person's natural gifts and abilities are and if they are a good fit for the role you are looking to fill.

Here are a couple of tips on DISC to help you fast-track the implementation of this game-changing communication tool. Look for clues. Again, people naturally leak "who they are," and as we mentioned, they have a deeply rooted need to be seen, heard, and connected to. DISC is our gateway into the human soul.

Here is a sample ad that Sarah wrote for an administrative position. Notice the "buzz words" designed to attract the "S/C" personality (you would not actually include the letters of DISC if you were to run this as an ad).

> *"We are seeking a full-time position with flexible hours. We need a personal assistant that is qualified to perform all areas of*

*administrative **support (S)** as well as learn real estate specific duties. If you are an **efficient (C)** person who is looking for a **long-term (S)** career position that is both **stable (S/C)** and **fulfilling (S/C)**, we look forward to talking with you. Must be **organized, (C)** have **good communication skills (S)** on the phone and in-person and proficient in Microsoft Office programs such as Word, Excel and Publisher. Salary ranging from $14-18/hour. Please write a letter explaining why you are interested in the position and include a PDF version of your resume, listing your experience and references. Send both to (email address) and please reference the word ASST **(demonstrates their reading skills)** in the subject line of your email."*

If you are hiring for a buyer agent or a listing partner, a combination of an "I/D" or "I/S" are perfect personalities for sales positions. Stay away from high "I's" for positions that require a lot of details, data, spreadsheets, etc., as illustrated by the story referenced above. Likewise, as it applies to the "D" personality when the job requires customer service, it's not that "D's" don't care about how people feel … they just don't have time to care!

If you are a team leader and you are a strong "D," you may want to shy away from hiring another strong "D" on your team for a sales position, as you may butt heads with two people battling to be in charge. ("D's" are typically natural-born leaders.)

When working with clients and applying the DISC personality tools, here are a few quick tips you can start using today:

D – Check the handshake. If it's firm with direct eye contact, you are encountering a "D." Mirror their fast pace, don't make decisions for them, and keep conversation to the main points. Their mantra is, "What is the bottom line?"

I – Do they have a wall full of photos of themselves doing cool things? The "I" loves to be the life of the party and gets bored easily with mundane tasks. Appeal to their flair and keep it fun and engaging. Their mantra is, "Enough about you; let's talk about me!"

S – Check their car. Is it a minivan filled with soccer balls and toys (for pets and kids)? Match their slower pace and reserved body language. Ask how they will build the business first before you jump into the business at hand. Their mantra is, "Can't we all just get along?"

C – Check the handshake. This time you are looking for a handshake that is not firm as well as intermittent eye contact. If you are in their home, open the pantry or a closet and look at the extreme organization. They may not have any photos on the walls or very few. Be accurate and on time. Let us repeat that: be accurate and on time! Their mantra is, "How does it work?"

If you google DISC personality assessments, you will find a few free resources online. To purchase a copy of your assessment with the additional Motivators Tool (another assessment that gives you a deeper comprehension of your personal motivators), you can do so at: WORKMANSUCCESS.COM/PURCHASEDISC.

"Never underestimate the power of intention."

~ Cheryl Richardson

It was Never a Perfect Week

Life is not perfect; it's messy and complicated.

When we call this amazing, game-changing tool, the Intentional Week, "perfect," we are inadvertently creating a major impediment in the execution. Most of us are pretty good at creating a calendar, but we are afraid to live it because what if it's not—you got it, "perfect?"

From now on, we will be referring to the concept of the "perfect week" as an "Intentional Week" because that is really what we are doing—using intention to leverage our time to maximize our output—which leads us to live a life of freedom. In other words, this is your magic pill.

It took Nate about thirty years to really embrace the Intentional Week. At one point, he admits it was too much accountability.

But his calendar management changed through coaching and becoming a Workman Success Systems coach. When he had to teach one of Workman's key concepts to the agents and brokers he coaches, it started to make more and more sense.

The biggest shift happened when he put his calendar everywhere he needed to see it. Now, there is a copy in his day timer, daily journal, on his computer, and in his phone. He gives it to his assistants and team—but most importantly, he has created an overlay in his Google calendar, so when he schedules an appointment, he sees the time blocks according to his Intentional Week. Seeing those blocks everywhere in his life caused him to shift his behavior to be in alignment with his intentions.

It was not easy to change the habit of being reactive but having the plan in front of Nate in his calendar made it far easier to abide by it in real life. Now it's ingrained in him, and he knows without looking where he has to be every day of the week.

Why the Magic Pill?

We decided to call this chapter Our Magic Pill because living by an intentional schedule is exactly that. It is a magic pill that solves a huge challenge that agents have in this industry: time management.

Today, Nate attends his youngest daughter's school and extracurricular activities, he golfs almost every Friday and travels more, and since implementing the Intentional Week, his team has consistently closed more transactions year-over-year.

We often talk about creating leverage in our business through systems, processes, teams, vendors, etc., but the simple yet highly impactful tool, the Intentional Week, is overlooked. Maybe because it seems too simple to create that much value, maybe it is too much accountability. Maybe it's because we've been calling it the wrong name all this time.

But it's worth repeating: Nate has made more money since he has started living by his Intentional Week, which means he can do more for his community and clients. He is now present with his family, does more of what he wants to do, and has seen more of the world than he ever dreamed possible. Talk about creating leverage in both business and life!

> ***"Time isn't the main thing. It's the only thing."***
>
> ***~ Miles Davis***

What if You Really had Enough Time?
"I don't have enough time" is a limited belief that many real estate agents subscribe to, but we'd like to challenge you to answer two tough questions:

- *Do you know how many hours a week you actually work?*
- *Are those hours spent on fake work that makes you look busy?*

As we mentioned in a previous chapter, 75% of the time that it takes for a real estate transaction to close is spent on non-dollar-productive activities. Yes, the home inspection is necessary for the property to close, but it is not, in fact, an MMA (money-making activity). That leaves us with a mere 25% of our day to do the most important thing we need to do in this business: prospect.

This is why it is essential that you hire an assistant after you sell your first home.

Better yet, if your brokerage has a company transaction coordinator, hire him or her before you write your first deal. Learn to delegate what is not the highest and best use of your time.

> **Here's a spoiler alert: unless it is finding new prospects to do business with you, it is not the highest and best use of your time.**

You might be arguing in your head that you are the *only* person the client wants to hear from. Well, we know that is just an excuse to hide the deeply rooted control freak that resides in your head.

Learn to delegate.

It will be the best thing you ever do for your business.

If you struggle with delegation, here are two tips for you.

- One, trust. You must trust the person you are relinquishing control to. You can't delegate if you don't trust them in a foxhole with you.
- Two, training. If you are confident they know what they are doing and that they are an extension of you in the business, delegation becomes easier (notice we said "easier." Delegation is hard, but it's a critical skill to learn if you want to dominate any real estate market).

Before we explore what an Intentional Week looks like, it is important to identify where you spend your time. The four categories that make up the week, Lead Generation, Lead Conversion, Client Care, and Personal Development, will help you do that.

Challenge each task.

Is it necessary?
Is it an MMA?

When we started selling real estate, the sexy buzzword in personal development was "time management." But we've since learned that time management is an oxymoron. We cannot change the fact that there are only twenty-four hours in a day. The sun comes up, and the sun goes down, and there are always the same hours in the day. But we can change how we choose to behave and the activities we focus on during the hours that we are "working."

What Are You Worth?

Do you know what you are worth per hour?

As Nate was growing up in the real estate industry, he loved installing his yard signs. He was so good at it that he made the signposts in his garage. When he came out of the construction industry, *he thought, why would I* *pay someone $30 to install a sign?* So, instead, he bought a post-hole digger and the lumber to build the signposts—even though he had to pay a buddy a six-pack of beer to borrow his truck because he didn't have one.

What he realized, after making a little bit of money selling real estate, was that while he was good at installing signs, it made much more financial and time sense to delegate it to someone else.

That's what we mean when we say that you have to challenge the dollar cost of each activity and identify (honestly) whether or not it should be done by you or delegated out.

> *"Money is not the key asset in life; time is!"*
>
> *~ Gordon Gekko*

Recently, Nate saw an agent post on Facebook about how her washing machine broke on the day she and her family got back from vacation. Of course, she had a ton of laundry to do. He has not done laundry in years because he learned to delegate. A lady does all his laundry. He stuffs a bag with as many clothes as possible, and she washes them for $25.00. Then he gets them back folded within twenty-four hours. It would take Nate hours to do laundry—and his hourly rate is far more than $25.00!

Another great example is an agent who spends half his Saturdays mowing the lawn. When we were looking for areas in his day-to-day life where he could find more time to prospect, it was suggested that he ditch the yard work. He shared that it would cost roughly $300 per month to have it serviced, which is $3600 per year—that was not in the budget. He really wanted to be done with his work, chores included, so he could have Sundays off to spend with his daughter on the lake in his backyard. The question he needed to answer was: is your daughter worth the $300 per month?

On a Facebook Live, John Assaraf, an author, speaker, business growth expert, and brilliant human being (you may have seen him in the movie, *The Secret*), was talking about this exact topic – how to have better time management and delegation. He talked about challenging every aspect of his day and how he added two hours to his week by changing how he got his hair cut. He lives in the LA area, and on average, it took him one hour to get to his barber, thirty minutes for the appointment, and another hour to get back to his office.

He asked if, for an extra charge, his barber could instead come to him weekly to cut his hair. The barber agreed to it, and it cost him slightly more for the service, but John could justify the expense because the two hours he gained were far more valuable. He also wears the exact same business attire each day because it saves him prep time in the mornings. That might be a little boring, but it *is* a highly effective use of time management.

Let's go a step further with this concept with a story from Sarah.

"My significant other and I were heading to Costco, and I told him to put hard-boiled eggs on the list. Now, if you shop at Costco, you know they sell perfectly cooked hard-boiled eggs that are already peeled and ready to go. I am not a cook, so I usually end up with half an egg white and an undercooked yolk when I attempt to make hard-boiled eggs. My partner challenged me, saying the ready-made hard-boiled eggs were not worth the cost and that buying a flat of raw eggs was a better deal at Costco. When I explained to him the amount of time it takes to boil the eggs, mess around with peeling them to get half an egg, and my frustration at the end product, the cost paled in comparison – especially when you consider my hourly rate."

> **Learn to challenge and delegate every task, even if it's as small as boiling an egg.**

So, how did Nate learn to delegate? Through his mentor, the great Howard Brinton. Howard used to tell a story about a guy who owned a pet pig and how every day he trained the pig to do tricks. Eventually, the pig responded on command to the man.

One day, the guy decided to take the pig to a bar. The bartender said, "Hey, you can't have a pig in here!" But the man said, "This is no ordinary pig. This is a special pig."

The bartender asked what he meant by "special pig." The man responded, "Watch this!" and on command, the pig jumped up, spun around, and then sat back down. The bartender was shocked and asked the man, "How long did it take you to teach that pig?" The man replied, "I worked with this pig every day for a year." "Isn't that an incredible waste of time?" asked the bartender. The man looked at the bartender and replied, "What's time to a pig?"

The moral of the story: next time you are doing something that should be delegated, just look at yourself in the mirror and make a little oink sound!

Step Three: Create an Intentional Week and Put it Everywhere.

An Intentional Week is effective, proactive, and ensures that you are productive in the hours that you are committed to working.

It is simply a schedule that, in an ideal world, could be executed flawlessly. But what does that *really* look like? Well, what are your big rocks? We discussed some examples at the beginning of this chapter. Other big rock examples might be taking part in morning routines such as the Miracle Morning™, volunteering, going on vacation, or attending or coaching kids' sports or other activities, etc.

Sarah has been going to the same lady to do her hair since 1994—that is a serious long-term relationship (the ladies reading this get it!). In all those years, she has only missed two appointments with her, and when it is on her schedule, she doesn't feel guilty or panic if someone wants to schedule an appointment with her during that time. She is simply not available, and no one needs to know why. This is a non-negotiable activity in Sarah's schedule.

> *"A man who dares to waste one hour of time has not discovered the value of life."*
>
> *~ Charles Darwin*

The Word "Try" is an Excuse in Advance

Without an Intentional Week to schedule your day around, you will continue to be sporadic and reactive in your life, both personally and professionally. If you say to yourself, "I am going to try to do (fill in the blank)," it will most likely not happen because you did not intentionally create time for it.

If you are just starting out, please don't confuse hard work and hustle with taking weekends off.

We both worked a lot of long days, weekends, and even major holidays in the beginning. However, as we matured and started to figure out the sales game, we realized we probably didn't have to do that if we put a plan in place like an Intentional Week.

If you are clear about your value proposition, the clients you serve will appreciate and respect your schedule. If you are good at what you do, you will be in great demand, and the customer will figure out how to meet with *you* during the week, during the day or when *YOU* are available.

Time Blocking; the New Sexy Word for Time Management.

Time blocking should be used to identify the four most important categories in a real estate business: generating new business, converting, servicing the client, and personal development/training.

The first two go hand-in-hand (but keep in mind that prospecting is defined as looking for new business and is not to be confused with lead follow-up or chatting up your bestie on the drive to the office).

Time blocking should be done in 30-45-minute intervals, and if you are a high "I" personality (from the DISC personality assessment tool), then we suggest you start with thirty minutes and give yourself a break to walk around the office, watch a funny cat video on YouTube or clear your Instagram notifications. Don't set yourself up for failure when it comes to time blocking. Be realistic about how long you can stick to one activity. Turn off your phone or put it on silent to minimize distractions. Put a do not disturb sign on your office door during your prospecting time block.

In the book *Higher Performance Habits: How Extraordinary People Become That Way*, author Brendon Burchard writes about the science behind time blocking. He notes it has been proven that the adult attention span is fifty minutes and furthermore, a 10-minute break actually refreshes and refuels the physical energy levels in the body, as well as the mind.

To put this in perspective, if you block one hour for prospecting, take a break for fifteen minutes and move your body. Go for a sprint around the office. Do some yoga moves or light stretching. It helps with your energy levels and attitude, so you are more effective and productive throughout the day.

Another huge challenge we see when coaching agents is the lack of consistent prospecting, and yet prospecting is the most critical activity we do in real estate sales.

If you want to be successful in dominating the real estate market, you must consider prospecting a big rock and intentionally put it on your calendar as a non-negotiable activity.

Stay engaged the whole time, and when you are finished with the block of time, assess how it went.

- *What can you do better next time?*
- *What did you learn?*
- *What was the result of the activity?*

When prospecting, always end on a high note. If you get that guy on the phone who tells you all REALTORS® suck, make one more call even if it results in leaving a message on voice mail. In the book, ***The Greatest Salesman in the World***, Og Mandino writes, "Every nah gets me that much closer to the yah." Don't be afraid of the rejection because those no's get you that much closer to the one who will say yes! We challenge you to keep prospecting until you get an appointment booked. #THATSTRUEHUSTLE

The Process

When you create your Intentional Week, put your big rocks in first. Then time block the four categories of a real estate business that we discussed earlier: Lead Generation, Lead Conversion, Client Care, and Personal Development. Leave time for listing appointments, buyer showings, home inspections, follow-up, and client care. Allocate each hour of your day to maximize your results.

Both of us use a Google-based calendar format, as mentioned earlier, but you can go as simple as a grease board hanging in your office or an old-school paper calendar. Whatever systems you use should be the best system for your business—just remember to keep it everywhere you need to see it!

If you have an assistant, make sure you share the calendar with them, as well as with your spouse and family. We both use color codes to indicate different activities. For example, an MMA might be in a green block because, you know, green for money.

Thank you, Hal Elrod, for Writing the Book The Miracle Morning

We also both follow the concept taught in the book *The Miracle Morning*, which describes a morning routine that follows an outline called S.A.V.E.R.S. If you were to study some of the most influential and successful people in the world, in any industry, you would find they all have one thing in common, and that is how they start their day.

We both can speak to the fact that the days we start by checking cell phone notifications first thing in the morning are the days that go to hell quickly. The cell phone is an amazing piece of technology, but it is a curse in being proactive and intentional. Still, you probably can relate if your cell phone is your alarm clock. That's the easiest way to get sucked into notifications first thing in the morning if you aren't disciplined. Here's a tip: buy an alarm clock; they still make them.

In *The Miracle Morning*, Hal talks about starting your day by filling your mind, body, and soul with good stuff. By good stuff, he means learning, mediation or prayer, gratitude, and visualizing the life you want to live, both personally and in your business.

The first hour of the day is critical. Starting out reactively to an email notification is not being intentional toward becoming the very best version of you that you can be. If you want to dominate any real estate market, you must live by intention; you must be on a never-ending pursuit to better yourself and your craft.

We don't want to steal any of the credit for the concept that Hal wrote in his book, so if you haven't read it yet, get a copy and check it out. Hal also has many spin-off books around the concept of *The Miracle Morning*, including one for kids and REALTORS®. You can also Google the acronym S.A.V.E.R.S. to learn more or join his community Facebook page.

> **"We are what we repeatedly do. Excellence then is not an act, but a habit."**
>
> *~ Aristotle*

There is much to be said about habits and how they relate to our success or lack thereof. Creating an Intentional Week is the only way to be in control of your time and ultimately expand your efficiency and opportunities as a real estate professional.

> *You have to work smarter, not harder. But we get it; change is not easy; and most likely will be messy.*

Be prepared for resistance and for all hell to break loose once you commit to working a plan. But know that it is perfectly normal to have setbacks and maybe even feel a little rebellious. You are normal, and most of us hate change, no matter how much we say we want it.

When you make this big change, challenge yourself to live your Intentional Week for seven consecutive days, no matter what is thrown at you. You will see your life begin to shift.

Big rocks, prospecting, an Intentional Week, all these tools boil down to creating good habits that you execute without hesitation. Every. Single. Day. What you do or don't do today doesn't have an impact on your business in that moment, but remember, 45-60 days from now, you *will* feel the impact. If you want to build a consistent and profitable work-life balance, implement an Intentional Week, and live by it without negotiation.

Executing the Intentional Week and effectively time blocking has given us our lives back. It has bought us freedom and leverage that we never realized it could have.

We knew it worked; people told us it did, but it was hard to believe them. We had to see it start to work in our lives before we really got it.

It has created space for other opportunities in Nate's life as well, like buying out his long-time business partner so he could retire and opening a Motto Mortgage franchise. In 2019, Nate had his best year ever, grossing just shy of $2 million GCI. Using these time management tools is like a magic pill.

Recap Step Three: Create an Intentional Week and Put It Everywhere.

Have some fun by using different colors to identify specific time blocks (like pink for date night or green for prospecting). Your first go at it will not be your last, so give yourself space to edit and make changes, but limit your time, so you don't get caught up in analysis paralysis! And don't forget, make sure you commit to working it for seven consecutive days before you make your first edits. Remember, there is no such thing as "perfect!"

Now that we have covered how to create a work-life balance in a thriving real estate business, it's time to shift our focus to what will make your phone ring. We'll see you in the next chapter!

- 7 -
Love the Hell Out of Your Database

"People influence people. Nothing influences more than a recommendation from a trusted friend. A trusted referral is the holy grail of advertising."

~ Mark Zuckerberg

A few years ago, Sarah was coaching a gal from the Midwest, and when she asked her where she kept all her contacts from the past thirty-five years of selling real estate, she told Sarah some were written down in a notebook, and the rest were on a floppy disk. Sarah joked that they'd have to take a trip to the local thrift shop to see if they could find a computer old enough to read a floppy disk. (Maybe you don't even know what that is!)

Sarah also worked with a client that had been building luxury custom homes for more than twenty-five years; she was there to help them brainstorm on how to market and get more business. They had a gorgeous storefront building right in the heart of the town where they were located, so Sarah suggested throwing a holiday open house/party in their building that would allow them to invite all their past clients. The three gentlemen looked at her as if she had two heads and admitted they had no contact information for the homes they had built in a client care management system.

Understand, we are talking about $750,000+ homes they had built over the course of more than twenty-five years. There were hundreds of homes and no way to track them—short of driving the streets to identify which homes they had built.

Those relationships and any future business were lost because they failed to track the homes they built and keep in touch throughout the year.

Step Four: Identify the Top 50 People in Your Life Who Love You, Trust You, and Have Either Done Business with You or Would if You Asked Them To.

The lifetime value of a client is $65,000 (or more).

Let's talk about a concept called "Top 50." This is a spreadsheet of fifty people who know you, like you, and/or have done business with you multiple times, as well as sent you referrals throughout the year. We call these raving fans.

To take it a step further, someone who is evangelical about you, who doesn't do business without you and won't let anyone they know do business without you, is a raving fan. A Top 50 relationship doesn't always have to be a past client; it is someone who supports your business by sending you referrals. And that can (and should be) lenders, other agents, vendors, etc.

To start your Top 50 list, identify who has done more than one transaction with you and who has referred you the most. If you are new and don't have any "past clients," then start with your family, friends, and general sphere of influence (SOI). If you don't think you know fifty people, put this book down now and grab your phone. Then go to your Facebook account or Instagram and click on your friends' list. Are there more than fifty? If you answered yes, you can build your database using your social media accounts.

You don't need leads; you need relationships.

The most successful people in sales, not just in real estate, have figured out that relationships are the most important asset in their business.

There are three things a consumer looks for in a transaction, and those are: Do they like you? Do they trust you? Do you know what you are doing? (That last one is optional since if they like you and trust you, they will still use you.)

Furthermore, high-performing agents will also tell you that the business they generate from their relationships is far more profitable than any online lead-generation options they take part in. In fact, these relationships are by far the most profitable lead-generation tool we have in the industry and in our arsenal. The idea or goal of a Top 50 is to always be in front of these people, so you are the first and only one they think of when it's time to make a move or when they hear of someone they know making a move.

The Top 50 list is designed to be organic and will change from year to year depending on who refers you and who doesn't. But before you kick someone off your Top 50 list, you need to find out why they have not referred you anyone lately. You can't assume they just don't know anyone to send your way because the average person knows five people who are ready to make a move in the next twelve months.

If you haven't gotten any referrals from them, you need to take a deeper look as to why and be honest about the answer.

Most of the time, when this happens, it's because the agent hasn't stayed in touch as much as they thought they had—they haven't been honest with themselves about their efforts to maintain and get referral business. Many agents are also afraid to call their database for fear of coming across as desperate, needy, or greedy. This leads to neglecting the future relationship and no referrals coming in.

If you are reading this book and are new to the business, you have a great opportunity to work smarter, not harder. It's okay that you don't have past clients to put on a Top 50 yet—you still know people who like you, trust you, and would do business with you if you asked. Don't assume because you are a little green that they won't hire you … until you ask.

If you don't ask, you don't eat.

Keeping track of each sale, referral, birthday, anniversary, milestone, and conversation is vital not just for maintaining relationships but in taking your relationships to the next level—which is where the gold lies in any database. Keeping good records is one part of managing your database but keeping it clean and current is as important. Your database is vital in helping you leverage future opportunities.

Let's explore a few of those opportunities.

After a transaction closes, our goal with the client is to be their go-to for all things real estate-related. We want them calling for a recommendation for anything they need when it comes to their home—which covers a lot of areas in a person's life.

> *"People don't care how much you know until they know how much you care."*
>
> *~ Theodore Roosevelt*

If you could refer a client to a reputable insurance agent who saved them a ton of money on car insurance when their child turned sixteen, or a trustworthy pet sitter when they finally booked that dream vacation they told you about, or a qualified estate planner when their parents moved to assisted living, you have done more than just help them with a home purchase or sale. You have impacted their life. That is where the magic happens—and it is how you create lifelong relationships in a referral-based business.

> **The greatest compliment we can receive is the referral of a family member or friend.**

Track Those Referrals!

Top-notch CMRs on the market today have features that allow you to track who has sent your referrals throughout the year. If you are in the market for a CRM or an upgrade, make sure you do the research to find a CRM with the best, most relevant features for today's technology.

When we started selling real estate, there were maybe a handful of CRMs out there. Nate's first database was a Rolodex, and Sarah used an index box—they might have been old school, but they worked.

Don't get stuck in analysis paralysis because you want to pick the "best" CRM on the market. None of them are perfect, and some will have features you like versus others you don't. They are all good, but the best one for you is the one you will use. If you don't own a CRM now, or have a freebie through your brokerage, go get one today.

If you don't know where to start, join our Facebook group. Just search *8 Ways to Dominate Any Real Estate Market*. Drop us a comment, and we'll give you a few suggestions to get you going in the right direction.

Tracking referrals is only one component of managing your database. It is vital that when you receive a referral from a past client, Top 50, family member, or friend, that you acknowledge the referral with a thank you. The client and the lead will determine what is an appropriate thank you—a referrer for a $100,000 buyer might not receive the same thank you as a referrer for a million-dollar buyer. Additionally, someone who has sent you multiple referrals may also require a high-quality thank you. So why not take that a step further by "squeezing the orange?"

Consider what happens when you squeeze an orange; it produces juice. If you squeeze the orange a little more, you get more juice. So how does that apply to a real estate referral? The concept of "squeezing the orange" means that you take the thank you to the next level.

For example, let's say you want to send an edible arrangement to a client as the thank you gift. Instead of delivering it to their home address, have it sent (or drop it off) at their place of work. If they work in a corporate or office setting, you will get the attention of their co-workers, and the conversation will go something like this: "Geez, my agent has never sent me anything like that!"

Or let's say your clients are Cardinals' football fans, and you want to acknowledge them with tickets for the next big game. Instead of just giving them tickets, go with them to the game. This is a prime opportunity to bond and deepen the relationship, which ensures future repeat and referral business.

You can implement thousands of ideas as appropriate gifts for your referral business. Whatever it is that you decide to do, take it to the next level to create a WOW experience for your SOI by "squeezing the orange."

Gen X and Gen Z

As an industry, we are missing a lot of opportunities in our databases because we aren't intimate enough with our relationships or the data our CRM provides.

Nate and I both struggle with this. I don't think there is an agent on the planet who doesn't. It's just the nature of the business. We get too busy working on what is in front of us that we neglect past relationships.

We either don't know enough about them personally and/or

professionally, or we have the data but aren't paying attention to it. Let's look at an example of where we might be missing the gold in our databases that concerns Gen X and Gen Z.

There is a high likelihood that your Gen X clients now have adult children who are ready to leave the house, whether they are off to college or staking out on their own for the first time.

A recent article published by RISMedia reported that 80% of Gen Z's have a goal to own a home before they turn 30; however, they are misinformed on how much money they need for a down payment.[1] We feel that a family with two Gen Z children living at home equals four possible transactions: two first-time homebuyers, one listing, and an additional opportunity when mom and dad use their equity to downsize into a smaller home. Think about how many Gen X clients you have in your database. How many transactions could you create by paying attention to the details?

Make it a goal to be this diligent with your data and the relationships you have, and you will never have to worry about where your next closing is coming from.

> *"If you believe business is built on relationships, make building them your business."*
>
> *~ Scott Stratten*

In the Phoenix market, we literally have every online investor buyer program available to us, including Zillow Instant Offers, as well as Zillow now competing as a brokerage. As they expand their foothold across the U.S. housing market, our database and the relationships with our clients will be at risk if we don't stay in constant communication and provide irreplaceable and relevant value to their life, both in and outside of an active real estate transaction. It is critical that agents stay on top of their databases and keep in touch with the people they know and with who they have done business!!

<u>People have</u> an innate need to be seen, heard, and understood, and they

---

[1] Campisi, Natalie. "Gen Z: Not-so-Easy But Worthwhile Steps to Home Ownership." *ACESocial*. RiseMedia, February 10, 2019. https://rismedia.com/2019/02/10/gen-z-homeownership/.

literally put their lives out there for the world to see through social media. What used to take years to learn about a person is available within seconds right from your smartphone (thank you, Mark Zuckerberg). Social media gives us valuable insight that we can use to deepen relationships and build trust quickly.

It also gives us the opportunity to stay relevant and dialed into the day-to-day happenings in our client's world. Before, it was a big task to stay in the know, but today, we can spend five minutes on Facebook and know exactly what is happening in their lives. We can take that a step further and use what we see happening as an opportunity to connect. For example, if someone posts that they are going to be empty nesters, it could result in the possibility of three transactions and an opportunity to drop off a book on how to successfully navigate becoming an empty nester. We can then educate them about how to utilize the Kiddie-condo FHA program so they can create an opportunity to build their wealth or start their child's wealth building through real estate ownership. Plus, mom and dad will want to downsize so we can list their home and help them find their perfect retirement house.

Remember, you don't need leads; you need relationships. The relationship starts the moment you meet; however, the gold doesn't come from the day you cash the commission check. That's just the beginning. The real gold lies in the longevity of the relationship.

Never forget that your database is king.

Recap Step Four: Identify the Top 50 People in Your Life Who Love You, Trust You, and Have Either Done Business with You or Would if You Asked Them To.

Now that we have injected into your DNA the vital importance of knowing who is in your database and staying in a consistent flow with them, we are going to share our marketing playbook. Heads up! You will want to bookmark the next chapter!

- 8 -
Lead-gen Like a Badass

"You are out of business if you don't have a prospect!"

~ Zig Ziglar

If you ask Nate if he prospects every day, he will tell you no. However, he does market his team and himself. Every day content print and digital advertising promotes his name so that the Phoenix market knows he is in business.

☙

In Nate's Words…

I was the guy who had nothing, and no one gave me anything. I learned early on to invest in my business, and I have always been the first to invest in technology. (I still do this even today).

When I was just starting out in real estate, I had one of the first portable computers, a Compaq with the original DOS-operating system and the awesome green screen and flickering fonts. It looked like the old-school salesman briefcase, and the front panel opened up to be the keyboard. I also bought the first portable 24-pin dot matrix printer that I hauled along with me (with the Compaq) to open houses.

It's remarkable that even though I was only twenty-six years old, I had a cutting-edge computer with a printer at my open houses along with flyers and comps on other homes. Yes, I was doing mega open houses before there was such a thing!

It helps that I have always been the guy looking for a better, more efficient way to do business—which inspired me to create a software that would auto-fill the old three-part HUD contracts. I hated to type, so I wrote a code that would move the cursor to the exact space to fill in the buyer's name, address, price, etc. This was a form-filled software long before the technology we have today.

I also wrote a software that qualified the people I met at open houses on the spot. The speed of a transaction was based on the knowledge I had, and I didn't want to wait on a lender to call them or have the prospect call a lender before I could sell them a house. I got it done right there. Oh, and I also brought along a four-inch black and white television. That wasn't for business. I just didn't want to miss the Cardinals games during my open houses.

☙☗

Early on in his career, Nate learned about direct mail from a CRS class; it was a game-changer for Nate and enabled him to dominate market share in the Valley of the Sun.

His first direct mail postcards were a horrid shade of peach and teal, but they were effective because they stood out. On the front side of the postcard was just one word like "SOLD" or "SUCCESS" accompanied by the Webster Dictionary definition. On the back was a little photo of Nate and the caption, "The Name You Know."

Those postcards, as basic and ugly as they were, did a lot for his reach in the community he worked. He has no doubt that thirty-five years later, they were a huge part of his success in this industry.

Let's digress for a moment and tell a story about another important decision that impacted Nate's career.

In 1989, when Nate was still a baby REALTOR®, he went to San Diego, California, to attend a Hobbs-Herder marketing event at the Hotel del Coronado. He was out of his league with the other top dogs in the room, not to mention he had never been somewhere so classy!

One of the speakers was Stanly Marcus, Nieman Marcus's son, who spoke about customer services, while Don Hobbs and Greg Herder talked about how to build the image of a successful REALTOR®.

Hobbs-Herder did a survey in a community with just a couple of simple questions along the lines of … If you were going to list your house with a REALTOR®, who would it be? What would you like in a REALTOR®? After they gathered the data, they built an eight-week postcard campaign based on the answers provided by those surveyed. They built a real estate "avatar" or, in other words, the "perfect REALTOR®"

based on the information the consumer said they wanted in an agent and then turned that into a market campaign that went out to those same folks they had surveyed. It's important to note, Hobbs-Herder marketed a fake person—the REALTOR® did not exist as a human being. However, after eight weeks of receiving the marketing postcard, they re-surveyed that same group of people, and the results were astounding. The majority of homeowners, who were asked the same questions during the first survey, reported they would hire the fake agent!

The presentation was so awe-inspiring that Nate *had* to sign up for Hobbs-Herder to build his brand and image through a brochure they created.

Even though Nate had no money, he believed in his gut that the brochure would be a great investment in his business, and he was right. It took action to go all-in and be fearless even though he was afraid (did we mention that Nate had no money?).

That decision set his local brand in motion. He gave Hobbs-Herder his credit card number, and they began the process of designing his personal brochure.

The Hobbs-Herder designer interviewed Nate and had him fill out a ton of paperwork. Literally, he had to provide a full background about his life.

Nate's vision for the brochure was to include the magnificent saguaro cactus—a king of the desert in Arizona, a real badass. The first edition of the brochure came back, and Nate's design had not been captured. What Nate got back looked like a 1970s tchotchke with a cheesy clip art photo of the desert. The boots and spurs portrayed were just not him and didn't match what he had in his mind's eye.

Nate wanted a dynamic photo of downtown Phoenix and the Sonoran Desert featuring the king of the desert. To give the designer a better idea of what he really wanted, he sent them the photo he wanted them to use to capture his idea, and the staff at Hobbs-Herder wrote the copy. When the mock-up came back the second time, it was spot-on: a polished, professional, personal brochure that signified a massive step up in his marketing game. It was through that brochure that Nate became "One of Arizona's Natural Resources."

The brochure was so good Nate was actually recognized by the National Association of REALTORS® (NAR) as having the best personal brochure in America, which created an opportunity for him to speak for NAR in Hawaii. The morning he was getting ready to leave, he was packing up his car with his bags and brochures when he spotted a note on his windshield.

It was a nasty-gram from one of Nate's neighbors accusing him of stealing her brother's personal brochure—he was an agent on the islands, and his personal brochure read, "One of Hawaii's Natural Resources."

As it turns out, Nate and his neighbor's brother had both hired Hobbs-Herder to design their brochures, and the writer on their staff was so moved by Nate's story that he copied it for this other agent! This was long before the Internet and goes to show what a small world we live in! Getting yelled at was worth it, though, because Nate ended up getting 10,000 postcards printed for free as an apology from Hobbs-Herder.

More Magic: Non-Stop Lead Generation

"Consistency isn't rocket science. Its commitment."

~ Unknown

Consistent lead generation is the lifeblood of a real estate business; however, it is something that very few REALTORS® master at a high level. The first step to accomplishing this is identifying your pillars, buckets, funnels, or whatever word you want to use to describe where leads come from.

The rule of thumb is to have four pillars, each generating 25% of leads. Your pillars must include your Top 50 or SOI, past clients, agent referrals, open houses, farming, expired listings, for sale by owners, and depending on where you are in your business; another pillar might include a paid lead platform like Zillow, Commissions Inc. (CINC), BoomTown, etc.

We believe that most agents leave a tremendous amount of commission on the table because their SOI pillar is weak. It is not enough to send out one holiday card and expect folks to remember you or be inspired to refer your services to their family and friends.

The easiest pillar to develop is your SOI and/or Top 50, and yet it is the pillar that gets neglected the most. Seventy-five percent of your business should be generated by your SOI.

Here's why.

As we touched on in the previous chapter, your SOI is defined by the people who know you, like you, trust you, and would do business with you if you asked them.

Your SOI is not exclusive to family and friends, but in many cases, those relationships need more nurturing and developing because, well, they are family and friends. If Sarah is working with someone close to her, like a friend or family member, she is giving them 110% customer service and client care because she never wants them to feel like she has taken their relationship for granted when it comes to their real estate needs. On the other hand, she has also referred a family member to another agent because she did not want to damage the relationship over a real estate transaction.

The goal is to identify fifty people in your SOI who like you, trust you, and would do business with you if you asked. They should be raving fans of you as a person and as a trusted real estate professional. These people have most likely done business with you and would never work with anyone else but you. Additionally, they would not let anyone they know work with anyone but you. These are the people we know, who support our business, year after year—if we develop and maintain the relationship. Your goal should be one referral per person in your Top 50 each year.

We can extrapolate that. The average person knows approximately 250 people in their life, and if that same person knows five people who will buy or sell a home in the next twelve months, do the math. That is a lot of freaking opportunities for you to help people buy or sell a home.

If you are reading this and thinking you don't have fifty people you would feel comfortable asking for business, please re-read the paragraph above and flip your thinking from a pushy and/or desperate salesperson to someone who is providing an important, valuable service. Actually, you are providing one of the primal needs: shelter. The goal isn't about asking for the business; the goal is to connect and build a relationship. The byproduct is the referral.

> *"Pretend that every single person you meet has a sign around his or her neck that says, 'make me feel important.' Not only will you succeed in sales; you will succeed in life."*
>
> *~ Mary Kay Ash*

People have a deep need to feel connected, appreciated, and understood—and they naturally want to tell us how we can do that. Intentionally look for ways to connect with your Top 50, such as giving them a book on how to plan a summer vacation in another country or how to become a first-time parent. Our goal with our Top 50 or anyone in our SOI is to be their conduit for *ALL* things real estate. We want them calling for a recommendation on anything they need when it comes to their home.

Check out this real-life example of how this works and the value of your Top 50 relationships.

In 1996, Nate met a guy we will call John through a sign call. Since then, he has personally bought and sold eleven homes with Nate. John's son has also bought a home from Nate's team. We have also helped his brother, nephew, racquetball buddy, and an employee at his insurance office. The relationship with John has generated over a quarter of a million dollars in commissions!

Step Five: Create a 12-month Written Marketing Plan, Implement, and Execute Consistently.

You know fifty people. Now go figure out who they are and call them.

As we mentioned above, one mailing during the holidays isn't going to build a John-type of relationship, especially during the time of year when people are inundated with holiday greetings from everyone else they know. So, what does a solid relationship-based marketing plan look like over a 12-month period?

Before we jump into what you should be sending out, let's review a few important tips to effectively create a marketing plan.

1. **Think Twinkie:** The Twinkie has no expiration date, which means it can sit on a grocery store shelf (or in your pantry) forever. When creating a marketing piece, you want to consider the shelf-life or how long your recipient will hang on to your marketing materials. A magnet, depending on what kind it is, could have years of shelf-life. A tin of cookies' shelf-life is only as long as it takes a person to devour them. Obviously, the longer the shelf-life, the better.

2. **What is the call-to-action?** What do you want your client to do when they receive the piece? Do you want them to call for a CMA (comprehensive market analysis)? Sign up for your newsletter? Come to an event? Call you for help?

3. **Who is my target audience?** Who is in your SOI and Top 50? Are they young families, retirees, or wealthy people? Remember, it's about what they want or need to receive from you as their real estate consultant for life.

4. **How often do they need to hear from you?** Every month, your database needs to receive something from you. At the minimum, they need to get a phone call from you quarterly. (If you really want to step it up, call your Top 50 every single month!). In addition, make sure you host plenty of client appreciation events, which we talk about in Chapter 10.

5. **How to communicate with them:** How to communicate with your clients is an evolving topic, and it depends on your database demographic. Advanced digital technology provides more options than just snail mail, including video, text message, and instant messages. But it is important to know how they want you to communicate with them. By the

way, email is the least preferred method of communication, per our clients (which is also your clients' feedback). So, if all you are doing is sending emails, you are doing exactly what they don't want you to do. Unless you are creating intentional content, tracking the open rates, and using a well-crafted email effectively with an extensive plan to get results—your client simply sees it as SPAM. They will delete it before even opening it.

The suggestions below are designed to help you create a 12-month marketing plan with tried-and-true ways to develop and deepen relationships with your clients. Also, at the end of this chapter, we have included a complete calendar of monthly ideas that will get your creative juices flowing!

- Monthly, quarterly phone calls
- Personal handwritten notes
- Birthday cards (coupled with a phone call, video message, text, or Facebook post)
- Pet birthday cards
- Anniversary cards (home anniversary and relationship anniversaries)
- Mother's Day, Father's Day, Grandparent's Day, Stepparent's Day, Pet-Parent's Day cards
- Valentine's Day cards
- Monthly newsletters
- Holiday card (could be any major holiday)
- Client appreciation parties (see Chapter 10)
- Coffee, lunch, dinner, tickets to an event, etc.
- Value-added gifts delivered by you (Brian Buffini calls this the "pop-by"); could be done monthly or quarterly.

Conveniently, a major event or holiday falls on nearly every month of the year. In addition, there are a lot of fun and whimsical "National Days" that could be used to create a marketing piece. If there are major events in your town, parlay off them by giving away tickets or using them creatively in your marketing verbiage.

Your marketing plan needs to be crafted each month and include a deadline of when you will start it and when it will be delivered. Strive to also work ahead a month, meaning if it is December, you would be working on January's marketing piece, and December's should have been done in November. Put the deadline on your calendar and stick to it. Better yet, find a way to delegate creating it if possible. Enlist the help of your lenders, title reps, and other vendors to help fill in the gaps where you need content. You'd be surprised what services are available if you just ask for help.

> *"Refuse to let the fear of rejection hold you back. Remember, rejection is never personal."*
>
> *~ Brian Tracy*

Calling Your SOI

A phone call is one of the most powerful ways to connect with your database, yet it is the one thing that an agent will avoid, even if it means they can't pay their bills or feed their children.

Sarah was on a coaching call the other day with a young lady in her early twenties, who was fairly new to the industry. She told Sarah she didn't want to call her friends from high school because she felt uncomfortable; she didn't want them to think she was trying to "sell them."

Sarah challenged her thinking by presenting a different way to look at calling her SOI. She said, "One day, your friends will get married and have a family. What if you helped them find their first home? And what if on the day they bring their first-born child home from the hospital, the threshold they cross for the very first time with their precious newborn is in the home that you helped them purchase?"

The young agent's eyes lit up. Sarah could tell she'd reached her.

As REALTORS®, we get to help a person (or a family) with one of the biggest financial decisions they will make in their life. More importantly, we get to help them with one of the most basic needs: shelter. We become a part of their story and their journey in life, and that is a privilege we should not take for granted. The relationship begins the day you meet, but the magic happens after the closing date.

Another Tool in Lead-Gen: Use the F.O.R.D. Dialogue to Build Rapport

Scripts and dialogues help us sound like professionals and overcome phone-call-phobia. An easy script that every person in the world uses, whether they are in sales or not, is the F.O.R.D., which stands for Family, Occupation, Recreation, Dreams. Think about it for a second; if you call your BFF, what is the first question you ask? Probably something along the lines of *how is the family? How is work going? What are you guys doing this weekend? How are the plans going for (fill in the blank)?*

We naturally ask these questions in our everyday conversations—and your neglected database is begging to have these conversations with you.

Deepening Relationships Through Social Media

Let's switch gears for a moment and talk a little bit more about modern-day relationship building with the invention of social media. In the past, it might have taken years to gain intel on a person you met at a party, open house, etc., but today, we have immediate access to intimate details through Facebook stalking. Remember, human beings have a deep need to be seen, heard, and connected to, and social media is a tool that we need to use to deepen our relationships with our SOI.

Pay attention to your client's/prospect's posts. If someone is complaining about their commute to work, it's a sign they could use your help. If they've just moved their last child off to college, that's another sign they could use your help.

The book, ***Swim with the Sharks Without Being Eaten Alive*** by Harvey Mackay, lists sixty-six questions you should know about your clients. Combine these questions with Facebook (the best tool ever designed to act as a voyeur into your client's home and life), and you will go a long way toward understanding your client and showing up where they are.

That's why Facebook is a billion-dollar company—people want to tell their stories, but the real question is—*do you want to listen?* Take advantage of the fact that people are putting their lives and needs out there for you to see—don't wait for them to solicit your services, or worse, call another agent. Pay attention to their posts, then reach out using the F.O.R.D. Script!

Badass lead generation is not rocket science. It is a commitment to consistently building relationships with people who know you, like you, and trust you.

Recap Step Five: Create a 12-month Written Marketing Plan, Implement, and Execute Consistently.

Here are annual events and suggestions to help you create your 12 months of touches ...

January Ideas:
- Happy New Year phone call using F.O.R.D.
- State of the Market letter and prediction for market conditions
- Closing Statement (send a copy of the closing statement to all clients the previous year to help them with taxes on January 10th)
- Annual mortgage and insurance review
- Birthday, anniversary, home anniversary cards
- Holidays: New Year, MLK Day, Chinese New Year

February Ideas:
- Superbowl bracket contest
- Valentine's pop-by (I love your referrals)
- Valentine's private dinner party for Top 50
- Host a blood drive
- Birthday, anniversary, home anniversary cards
- Holidays: Ground Hog's Day, Presidents' Day, Black History Month, Valentine's Day, National Random Acts of Kindness

March Ideas:
- Host a client event (March Madness or St. Patrick's Day)
- Lottery tickets to Top 50 (do you feel lucky? Or don't leave your home value's up to the luck of the leprechaun!)
- Call your SOI!
- March Madness bracket contest
- Birthday, anniversary, home anniversary cards
- Spring cleaning tips
- Pi Day (give away a pie or a coupon to a local bakery)
- Birthday, anniversary, home anniversary cards
- Holidays: St Patrick's Day, Spring Equinox, International Women's Day, Day Light Savings

April Ideas:
- Host an Easter egg hunt in a park—if you farm, host it in the farm area and invite the community
- Host a professional photo day for Easter
- April showers bring May flowers—want to know what your home is worth?
- Host a Shred-Event
- Birthday, anniversary, home anniversary cards
- Holidays: Easter, National Pet Day, Earth Day, Arbor Day

May Ideas:
- May Day themed pop-by (May 1st)
- Host a Cinco De May client party, Derby Day, or Memorial Day event
- Mother's Day cards and/or deliver flowers to Top 50
- Birthday, anniversary, home anniversary cards
- Holidays: Memorial Day, National Star Wars Day, Cinco De Mayo, National Wine Day

June Ideas:
- Host a movie event (pick a blockbuster and schedule on opening weekend for best ROI)

- Call your SOI!
- Tips on how to plan a family vacation
- Water safety tips
- Father's Day cards
- Birthday, anniversary, home anniversary cards
- Holidays: Flag Day, Father's Day, National Donut Day, Pride Month, Summer Solstices

July Ideas:
- Happy 4th of July pop-by (flags or patriotic pinwheels)
- Host a movie event (pick a blockbuster and schedule on opening weekend for best ROI)
- Host a concert in a park event—if you farm, host it in the farm area and invite the community
- Back to school tips—host a backpack donation drive for underserved communities
- Host a 4th of July event
- Host an ice cream social
- Birthday, anniversary, home anniversary cards
- Holidays: 4th of July, National Ice Cream Month, National Hot Dog Day, National Tequila Day

August Ideas:
- Dog days of summer pop-by if they have pets
- Host an end-of-summer BBQ
- Why fall might be the perfect time to sell your home
- Back to school tips
- Birthday, anniversary, home anniversary cards
- Holidays: Friendship Day, Dog Day, National Book Lovers Day, National S'mores Day

September Ideas:
- Happy Labor Day pop-by
- Call Your SOI!
- Host a client event
- Birthday, anniversary, home anniversary cards
- Holidays: Labor Day, Hispanic Heritage Month,

Grandparent Day, Fall Equinox, National Tailgating Day, National Beer Lovers Day

October Ideas:
- Deliver pumpkins to your Top 50 and have a carving contest
- Host a fall festival event
- Hand out candy and adult goodie bags on Halloween night
- Pumpkin carving contest or coloring contest
- Birthday, anniversary, home anniversary cards
- Holidays: Breast Cancer Awareness Month, International Coffee Day, National Taco Day, World Animal Day, Halloween

November Ideas:
- Do a pumpkin or apple pie give-away to your Top 50
- Thanksgiving Day holiday card
- Host a food drive or blanket drive
- Birthday, anniversary, home anniversary cards
- Holiday: Daylight Savings, Veterans Day, Thanksgiving, National Forget-Me-Not Day, Black Friday, Small Business Saturday

December Ideas:
- Host a Photos with Santa party
- Host a Holiday open house with drinks and appetizers
- Holiday card mailing
- Host a coat drive, toy drive, or wrapping paper drive
- Call your SOI!
- Birthday, anniversary, home anniversary cards
- Holidays: Pearl Harbor Day, Christmas, Channukah, Kwanza, Winter Solstice, National Chocolate Day

To dominate any real estate market requires a consistent, focused effort on the right activities. Now that you have a marketing plan that will make your phone ring, it's time to take your business to the next level.

Join us on our Facebook page at *8 Ways to Dominate Any Real Estate Market*. We'd love to see your marketing ideas!

- 9 -
Why We Celebrate Hitting Singles

"Your gal isn't to buy players. Your goal is to buy wins. And to buy wins, you have to buy runs."

~ Billy Beane

Despite a small budget, in 1981, the Oakland Athletics Baseball Team won the American League West division title by doing something that no ball club had ever done before. They studied team analytics and used a sabermetric approach ("SABRmetrics is the empirical analysis of baseball, especially baseball statistics that measure in-game activity."). This created a competitive, winning team. In other words, the A's made it to the playoffs by hitting single plays, not big home runs like other professional baseball teams were doing with a superstar lineup of players.

We wanted to start this chapter out with the story of Billy Beane, the former coach of the Oakland A's because it's an excellent, true-life example of how success can be achieved with consistent, focused efforts on the right activities, and it underscores that you don't need a big budget to make it to the playoffs year-after-year.

"If you can't measure it, you can't manage it."

~ Peter Drucker

Step Six: You Can Win a Baseball Game Hitting Singles, But the Only Way to Know if You Are is to Track Your Stats.

The Challenge of Our Industry

The real estate industry is unique because it never shuts off. It is with you every day, everywhere you go. It showers with you, eats dinner with you, goes to bed with you, and often that vacation you so desperately need is ruined because you have to work. It never shuts off, and that is why so many agents miss important milestones with their children and end up divorced, burnt out, and miserable.

The solution to this work-life balance challenge can be found through documenting and tracking every aspect of your business. How will you measure your success if you don't track it? How will you know when to course-correct if you are not tracking? How will you know what is working or not working if you are not looking at your business like a business?

As we mentioned in another chapter, 75% of each real estate transaction concerns non-money-making activities, which makes tracking your business that much more important. But what should you be tracking? And how often?

Years ago, Nate told his mentor and coach at the time, Howard Brinton, that he had a goal to golf more the following year. Howard asked Nate how many times he had played that year, but Nate couldn't tell him because he had not kept track of how often he was on the course. Howard asked him, "Well, how will you know if you play more next year?" Nate had to track it.

If you want to walk 10,000 steps a day, that's a great goal, but how will you know if you did it? How will you be accountable to yourself?

In this day and age, you would probably purchase a fancy watch that tracks every step you take—which is a start to becoming accountable. But what about taking another step to analyze how often you were active?

- *Did you hit the goal 70% of the time?*
- *50% percent of the time?*

Talk is cheap, but tracking ensures accountability, which ultimately leads to results. When you learn to track everything, you will succeed in dominating any real estate market.

> *"If one does not know to which port one is sailing, no wind is favorable."*
>
> *~ Lucius Annaeus Seneca*

Digging Into ROI

We touched on ROI (return on investment) but now let's really delve into what that means and what you should be tracking in your business. Anything you do more than three times needs a documented system and should be tracked to identify if it is working, if it needs improvement—or if it should be dumped altogether.

In 1998, when the Arizona Diamondbacks came to town, Nate was quick to sign up for an advertisement in their magazine. The full-page ad cost $24,000 but allowed Nate to upgrade his four-season tickets to a premium location behind home plate. This added perk has no price tag when Nate and his family recall the unforgettable memories of attending the World Series games in 2001 when the Diamondbacks won game seven of the series—the only World Series they have ever won as a baseball team.

The ad did not produce the real estate results we expected. We know this because we tracked the ROI. When we ran the ad a second time, we got the same results. That is *a lot* of money spent to generate zero return. The point of the story is to be clear on why you are making the decisions you are. That's why tracking is essential.

When we ran the Diamondback ad, Nate had already sold a house to Todd Stottlemyre, two-time World Series baseball champion. This was the spark that ignited the vision of working with more baseball players. Nate has always been fascinated by celebrity status and, in the real estate industry, has earned his fair share of the limelight. So why not up the game with famous baseball players as his clientele?

Todd was actually a RE/MAX referral, but Nate hoped that if he ran the ad, the players in the clubhouse would see the ad, and Todd would endorse Nate as his REALTOR®. It was Nate's ego that wrote the check for the ad, with a vision that he would meet and work with other big-time baseball players.

When they didn't call us, he saw the ad as a failure. Let's be clear: the ad did generate leads, but we were not prepared for the type and volume of those leads—especially those that came from outside our normal service area in the Valley of the Sun. We were not prepared to drive sixty miles to a listing appointment, nor did we know enough about the community amenities like the schools and hospitals, etc.

Nate has always been a very intuitive marketing genius, and in the case of the Diamondbacks ad, he was right … the ad did generate leads, but we left out a part of the plan. The part that called for us to manage the increased volume in an area we weren't familiar with. We were unrealistic about who the lead would be. It's important to use your gut to pull the trigger on big advertising ideas, but you need to have a plan to handle the results and be clear on the desired outcome.

The other lesson to take from that experience is not to be afraid to kill an advertisement if it's not working. As we shared earlier from the genius Albert Einstein, "The definition of insanity is doing the same thing over and over and expecting different results."

Well, you can apply this to your marketing. If it's not working, cancel it. The second takeaway is not to let your ego write the check. Advertising should be a calculated risk with a goal of at least three times the ROI.

Let's digress for a moment to tell a fun story about one of Nate's experiences with a famous baseball player that came about because of that advertisement … You'll see there were some benefits to this marketing endeavor after all.

Nate did rub elbows with a few professional players because of the Diamondback ad. And he did help one other player—outfielder Ichiro Suzuki purchase a few homes in the Valley of the Sun.

It was a normal Saturday in the office when Nate pulled up on his custom motorcycle dressed like he was just leaving a biker club meeting, wearing jeans with frayed hems, black Harley boots, a white tank top, dark sunglasses, and one of those belts that has a chain, so your wallet doesn't fall out during the ride.

Sarah popped out of her office to greet him and asked what he was doing at the office. His blue eyes danced with excitement as he replied, with a big Nate-style grin, "I am meeting Ichiro!" Sarah might have let out a slight gasp when she asked him, "Dressed like that?!?" Nate looked down at his attire, and she could see his excitement turn to regret and embarrassment.

He quickly made his rounds about the office to see if anyone would loan him a shirt to no avail. Time was running out. Within moments, Ichiro arrived at the office, and it was too late for a wardrobe change.

Ichiro, his wife, and their translator came in through the glass doors of the office to be greeted by a now nervous Nate. Sarah stood around the corner, feeling a little responsible for his current disposition based on her outburst of shock at his choice of clothing to meet such a famous client. But in a split second, the climate turned, and it is a moment that Sarah will never forget.

Ichiro pointed to Nate's bike parked outside the glass doors and, in his broken English, asked Nate if that was his motorcycle. Nate glanced at the floor, then sheepishly said, "Yes." Ichiro turned back to Nate and declared, "You a pimp, Nate!"

... Classic Nate

For a few years, Nate advertised at the Peoria Sports Complex, which is the annual spring training location for the Seattle Mariners, the team that Ichiro played for. It was a fence banner with our company name, RE/MAX Professionals. Every spring training game played at the complex; Ichiro stood in front of our fence advertisement. Little did he know then, Nate would later be his REALTOR®.

What is additionally cool about this story is getting to see our company name in the background of an awesome photo of Ichiro diving for a ball or making a winning throw that was replayed on the evening news, or that made the ESPN spring training highlight of the week. That was an experience we just can't put into words!

Sometimes advertising doesn't produce the results we hope for, but it presents us with other perks we didn't expect. Remember, we knew what worked and what didn't because we measured it.

If you want to figure out when and how to spend your money, track it!

Key Performance Standards That Need to be Tracked Daily, Weekly, Monthly, Quarterly, Yearly

Opportunities are defined as a chance to engage someone in a meaningful conversation about buying or selling real estate. This includes the cashier at the local grocery store who sees your nametag and asks you how the market is. A good rule of thumb is for every five outbound calls;

you should connect with one person. Your sphere of influence will have a better return on investment than other leads you are not as familiar with because they are more likely to answer your call than a cold internet lead.

Unique Ways to Create Lead-Gen Opportunities

You are a moving billboard, and so is your vehicle. Why not make it obvious what you do for a living? You will rarely see Nate without some kind of branded industry-relevant logo on his shirt, and Sarah wears a loud blingy name tag that is hard to miss. Even if you are not a RE/MAX agent reading this book, you can still take advantage of branded swag or a name tag to show off your business.

Sarah has used the power of the RE/MAX brand and swag to create new opportunities.

Sarah says …

I needed to buy a new laptop, so I headed to Best Buy, of course, wearing my RE/MAX logo name tag. The young kid who helped me purchase a new computer noticed my name tag—and, more importantly, the RE/MAX balloon. He proceeded to tell me that he and his wife wanted to buy a home. So, I took them out the very next week and sold them a new construction home. Had I not been wearing my name tag, that conversation may not have taken place.

So, buy a name tag at the very least, and consider purchasing other swag like a hat, shoes, socks, shirts, or accessories, etc.

Swag is a gateway to conversations.

We should always look for ways to find new opportunities to engage in a meaningful conversation about real estate, whether that is through a business card included with your tip at lunch or given to the cashier at your local grocery store. Don't be a secret agent!

Another great idea is coffee shop prospecting.

What is coffee shop prospecting?

Simply set up your office for the day at a coffee shop and pre-buy $100 worth of coffee (or whatever value you want to spend) and include with it a card that has your information on it. The idea is that you will buy people coffee throughout the day, and when the customer gets their coffee, they also get your card. Now, they know it was you treating them to their cup of Joe.

It's especially fun when the cashier gives the card with the cup of coffee to the person and then points you out to the surprised coffee drinker.

Of course, they will approach you to say thanks, and what do you think happens next? That's right, a conversation about real estate. The law of reciprocity—what this example explains, happens when a recipient feels obligated to return the favor to the giver or do something nice in return.

If you are farming, we highly encourage you to visit the local coffee shop if possible. If there is not a coffee shop in the area, pick another business where you could work this idea. The more people in the community who see your face, the better your farming efforts will be.

Conversations: An actual conversation is different than an "attempt." A real conversation should lead to a booked appointment in your calendar. If you're not booking a slot, then you may want to ask yourself if you are having real conversations. Most agents fail to sell enough real estate to pay the bills because they are not getting in front of enough people. We're talking face-to-face meetings or Zoom-to-Zoom calls. If you want to sell more real estate, book more appointments!

Appointments: Tracking how many people you meet with is critical. It helps you to identify your conversion rate and can be a measure of how effective you are at closing the deal. Remember, there are no bad leads, just people who might not be ready at that moment. It warrants repeating: if you want to sell more real estate, book more appointments!

TRACKING FOR LISTINGS

It is critical that you also track how many listings you take, how many successful closes you have, your average days on market, and what your percentage of list price to sales price is.

At one point, we knew our team was listing and/or selling a house every twenty-three hours. We had that stat put onto the plastic bags that we used to deliver our pre-listing packages because that is an important and impressive number. Plastering that message helped us convert more appointments into signed listing agreements.

Keep top-of-mind that sellers want to work with an agent who can help them with two concerns: how much money they will make and how long it will take to sell their home.

If you can demonstrate results, you will be in great demand as a listing agent. But the only way to know your stats (and if they are impressive) is by tracking daily, weekly, monthly, quarterly, and yearly data.

Even 30+ years later, Nate still tracks every appointment he goes on, whether he gets the listing or not. And he has started tracking those sellers who never put their homes on the market at all. That's because he has discovered another opportunity to be of service and create value if he follows up with those folks.

Tracking Marketing Using an IVR

For years we have used an IVR (interactive voice response) call-capture system to track our marketing efforts. Currently, we are using a service called VoicePad. On every sign we have in the ground, there is a sign rider attached that has a special phone number that can be called to receive recorded information about the home for sale, 24/7. We receive all the information about the caller's ID immediately, and they also have the option to speak with one of my team members from VoicePad.

It's important to note that we remove the price from the recorded information. We want them to press zero to connect with us to get the other details on the home. It's a great lead conversion tool.

We also use VoicePad to track our marketing pieces to see what is generating phone calls and what is not. For example, we market to a community in Peoria, Arizona, called Blackstone Country Club. In the monthly newsletter, we advertise that same IVR phone number with a 4-digit code the caller must use. That code is specific to the Blackstone advertisement, and we don't use it on any other marketing pieces. If that code is used by a caller, we know exactly which piece they are looking at. You can do this type of 4-digit code tracking with an IVR tool on all your marketing, listings, websites, signs, flyers, etc. When you're deciding where to spend your money on marketing, it's a real game-changer that makes the phone ring.

Tracking for Buyers

Working with homebuyers can be a time-sucking activity, especially in competitive markets, which is why tracking is vital. Again, it identifies your conversion rate and is a measure of your negotiation skills and closing abilities. A rock star buyer's agent should know how many houses they are looking at every week, the average amount of homes shown to one client before they write an offer, how many contracts are written, how many get accepted, and how many successfully close.

Tracking also needs to include the list price to sales price ratio, how many home warranties were negotiated, as well as the average closing costs negotiated in the buyer's favor. In any market, homebuyers want to work with an agent who can help them find the perfect home at the best price and terms. But the only way to know how awesome you are is through tracking daily, weekly, monthly, quarterly, and yearly.

Why is it so critical to track this information? We know you don't necessarily care how many home warranties you might negotiate in a year, but the consumer does because it tells a story about your worth as an agent.

For example, if you sold twenty-four homes, and on average, negotiated 1% off the list price, with an average sales price of $300,000, plus a $700 home warranty—that could be an average savings to your clients of approximately $3,700. *That* becomes your story. In other words, it is a part of our value proposition in the marketplace.

The Importance of Doing a Buyer Consultation

Let's digress for a moment to address an important step in successfully working with homebuyers. It makes us crazy when we hear about an agent running across town at 5:00 pm on a Friday to show one house; whether it is a sign call or a referral, the source doesn't matter. Consumers today think that buying a house is like what they see on the latest reality show on television; they have no clue the risk and potential pitfalls that they could face because reality television doesn't air that part unless it gets them better ratings.

If you want to gain the commitment and loyalty of more homebuyers, professional consultations have to become a non-negotiable part of your business. Unfortunately, this was a tough and costly lesson to learn.

The two times Sarah "skipped" a buyer consultation with a new client ended up being two of her worst nightmare transactions—and neither deal closed!

A solid buyer consultation sets the stage for a successful transaction and establishes trust in you as the expert. It makes it easier for the client to say yes to the house when you find the right property. Your consultation does not need to be overly complicated or include a flashy PowerPoint presentation (but you certainly can include it if you like that idea). If you are a RE/MAX agent, you have access to a beautiful digital or print option PDF in Megaphone™ on the RE/MAX Max/CenterGo that can be customized to you.

Ideally, a buyer consultation should be a face-to-face (or virtual) appointment at your office in a professional setting with all the parties who are involved in the buying decision.

The presentation is you walking them through the purchase contract line-by-line, explaining what it means to buy a house, and defining earnest money, and the fiduciary duties of an agent, as well as the contingencies, inspection, and repair process. You need to discuss all the ways they could lose their earnest money, and what happens the day they close. It also includes an explanation of the addendums and disclosures (which you want to have them sign if possible—to get them out of the way). This could also be a good time to get a buyer broker agreement signed. It is important to address new homes, open houses, and FSBOs with the client.

Get them to agree to the following:

1. Not attending an open house

2. Not visiting model home locations in a new subdivision

3. Not calling an FSBO

4. Not making any major purchases during the buying process

5. Not changing employers during the buying process

6. Not co-signing for another party

Lastly, explain what they can expect of you as their agent and your compensation for those services.

Good agents are in great demand by homebuyers, and the majority of buyers use an agent to find their home. If you can master this process, buyers will beg for your professional representation!

A final thought about buyer consultations—showing one house to a buyer doesn't make you money. Schedule a tour of homes and give the client permission to make a decision to ink a contract that day. One house here or there is a waste of time, especially if they are a legitimate buyer.

If you want to convert more buyers into happy homeowners (and fatten up your bank account with more commission checks), a buyer consultation is a must.

Conversion Rates

Basic math can help determine what an agent's conversion rate is. If you go on 100 listing appointments and land fifty of them, we know your conversion rate is 50%. The best-of-the-best are averaging around a 65% conversion, and some of the elite in our industry are ranking below that conversion rate. That sounds like an odd goal, but if you remember what we said earlier—that most agents fail to meet their goals because they don't go on enough face-to-face appointments, it is a goal most can understand. If you are at a 100% conversion rate, we take that to mean you are not going on enough appointments or are only selling to your family. Successful agents have figured out the more people they meet face-to-face, the more houses they will sell—which drives your conversion rate down.

Nate's nephew was a buyer agent on our team. He used the same script with every buyer he worked with, and probably eight out of ten times was successful. His script went something like this: "We are going to look at five homes when we go out Saturday. Based on what you have told me you are looking for, these are going to be the best five houses on the market that fit your needs. And you are going to buy one of them." Then he would take them out, show them five houses, and come back to the office to write up an offer. This was a closing skill he developed that resulted in a strong conversion rate.

When Sarah decided she wanted to teach and speak in public, she knew she wasn't very good at it and needed to improve, so she joined Toastmasters. The best tip Sarah learned in those few years was from the impromptu speaking portion of the meetings. That's when the "toastmaster" for the evening has a topic and throws out a question at random. If you get called on, you have two minutes to answer the question, but you have to use the word of the day to qualify, which makes it that much more challenging. You have to be quick on your feet and ready with a comeback at a second's notice.

Sarah had an epiphany one night after leaving Toastmasters; scripts and dialogues were like impromptu speaking. To be a quick, on-your-feet thinker meant you needed to pull a script out of thin air to overcome an objection or concern. Not only did Toastmasters help a person discover a solution in front of a client, but that solution made you sound polished and professional. A solid, well-rehearsed dialogue can help you convert and overcome difficult objections like commission or pricing.

Bruce Lee was quoted as saying he did not fear a man who knew 10,000 kicks but rather a man who had mastered one kick 10,000 times. Learning new scripts will sharpen your skills but practicing scripts will make you a rock star at converting leads.

*

While we are on the topic of conversion rates, let's digress to a humorous marketing story in our real estate journey …

It was just before the boom in the Phoenix market, so probably around 2002 when Nate was asked to speak on a panel at a local real estate one-day conference called the Duel in the Desert – it was a pretty big deal at the time in our local market. The panel was sharing their listing presentation with several hundred REALTORS® in a mock seller listing interview. Nate was competing with another well-known top producing agent in the Valley (you may know him from his famous television commercials, "If you're not happy, fire me."). He has a bit of a sense of humor and started right away with the trash-talk to throw Nate off his game at the conference, which was a part of the deal in marketing this event.

We were fiercely committed to maintaining our ranking as one of the top ten RE/MAX teams in Arizona—since we were typically number one. After a listing appointment, we would have a local flower shop deliver a custom team coffee mug filled with flowers to the homeowner as a thank you for letting us meet with them to discuss selling their home. We took this a step further if we knew they were interviewing other agents and would ask the potential seller what date and time the other agent would be there.

With that knowledge, we would then request the flower company to deliver the flowers at the exact same time they were interviewing the other agent. Tricky, yes, but effective for maintaining number one—and exactly what we planned to do to our competitor during his panel presentation.

At that time, Nate owned a 100-year edition Fatboy Lowrider Harley motorcycle, so we decided to record a video staged at an old mining town out in the West Valley Desert while incorporating the beloved RE/MAX hot air balloon.

We rented the balloon for a morning flight, and two of our employees pretended to be a seller client. They waved happily from the hot air balloon while they called out, "Thanks Nate, for selling our home!"

Then on Easter Sunday, Nate, Nate Jr., and Brandi (Nate's children), and Sarah drove out to the mining town to record part two of this elaborate comeback to the trash-talking.

The town was maintained by two old men who looked exactly like how you'd expect true grit minors to appear. They were tall and scraggly with sun-leathered skin, long wild gray beards, dingy white tee shirts, and oversized dusty jeans held up by suspenders.

Nate had to look the part, too. He wore a black Stetson cowboy hat and dressed like a version of Johnny Cash, black bandana, leather duster, and all—his outlaw bike acting as his trustworthy steed.

The old buildings and rickety wood porches surrounded by log fences, where many years ago, miners had tied up their horses when they came to town, were the perfect stage. At the top of one building was a sign painted in peeling white paint on sun-faded wood: "Land Sales Office."

We gave the two old miners a one-line script, which went something like this:

Miner One: "You know that Nate Martinez?"

Miner Two: "He's the best damn land salesman around."

Miner One: "Yep." (Then spits tobacco on the ground.)

They were not professional actors, so their one lines took a few takes to get right. But what fun it was capturing it on film! #HISTORYINTHEMAKING

The final line was Nate's. He turned to the camera after reeving the engine on his bike, pulled up a prop shotgun from his side that the miners had lent us, fired one shot, and said, "By the time I get done, you'll be pushing up daisies." Then he sped off down the dirt road leaving a cloud of dust behind him.

This was long before the technology we have today to create video content, so Sarah had to take the film to a filmmaker in downtown Phoenix to have it edited and spliced together. It took hours and cost way more than we should have spent on our comeback and trash talk coming from our rival. The depths we went to were ridiculous—it took so much time and cost hundreds of dollars—all to beat our competition. (Did I mention how competitive we were then?)

The final product started out with the infamous song *The Good, the Bad, and the Ugly* and ended with Nate riding off into the desert. It was not Hollywood-worthy but definitely real estate marketing brilliance!

On the day of the conference, the whole team attended to support Nate on the panel presentation. We asked the guys running the soundboard if we could play our video before the panelists began, and they happily obliged. The audience exploded in laughter when it was over, which set the tone for Nate's mock seller presentation.

But that wasn't all we had planned. We had a second request for the sound guys—a doorbell chime. Halfway through our competition's mock listing presentation, Sarah walked up to the stage and pretended to knock on a door while the sound guys played the doorbell chime. The third panelist pretending to be the "seller" wasn't quite sure what was happening, as none of this was scripted or on the agenda. Sarah then handed a tin bucket full of white daisies to the bewildered "pretend seller" and said, "Nate just wanted to say thank you for the opportunity to list your home." A second explosion of laughter resounded from the audience.

That's how you win a listing and maintain the number one spot.

TRACKING REFERRALS

We have taught you how to grow your referral business in previous chapters; now, let's talk about the importance of tracking all those new leads. Tracking your referral business gives us two vital pieces of intel in our database. It helps us identify who are our best raving fans (those who refer you the most), and it gives us an opportunity to find out why we aren't getting referrals from everyone else.

If someone is a rock star in your database and sends you a ton of referrals throughout the year, it's imperative that you don't neglect or take that relationship for granted. These folks need to be recognized and appreciated!

If someone has not sent you any business, this is a great opportunity to engage them to find out why and if there is anything you can do differently to earn their referral business. If they are never going to refer you, then reconsider their place on your "cool kid bus" when it comes to client events and the other perks you offer throughout the year in your marketing plan.

Tracking Leads

Workman Success Systems notes that an average listing gets 6-8 leads every thirty days it is on the market. Agents like to challenge this data but, in reality, have no clue how many leads they are generating because they are not usually tracking them.

Example:

Agent: "Hi, this is Jane Doe with XYZ Real Estate. How can I help you?"

Caller: "I am interested in the house you have listed at 123 Maple Street."

Agent: "That house is currently under contract."

Caller: "Okay, thank you."

Believe it or not, that was a lead, and Jane Doe just missed an opportunity to convert a prospect!

Every inquiry on any listing for sale, pending, or sold, is a lead, and it needs to be tracked.

This goes for paid advertising as well. If money is spent, the ROI needs to be tracked. Systems to track leads can be as simple as a spreadsheet or index cards if you want to go old-school.

There are plenty of affordable CRMs available today that track leads and contacts. So, pick one and use it religiously.

A note to team leaders: you will always be tracking leads and following up with your team members to make sure they are converting the leads into clients. If you are not, you are losing money. You will also always be holding your team members accountable for lead follow-up. If you are not, you are losing money, but worse than that, you are losing creditability.

If your leads are in your CRM, they need to be reviewed with the team a minimum of once a week. Maybe more often, depending on the dynamics of your current team environment.

If your leads are on a spreadsheet tracker, this document needs to be reviewed every single week with your team. That's non-negotiable. Otherwise, you are losing money.

At the end of the chapter, we will provide a link to our latest tool, *Your Real Estate Journey to Abundance: 8-Step Journal*, and a link to a basic sample of a lead tracker that you can implement if you are not currently using a system to track your incoming leads.

Lead Follow Up

In the last few years, we have seen an increase of ibuyers (internet buyers) and technology-based real estate companies taking a bite out of our industry. They exploit our lead follow-up weakness. According to NAR, the average homebuyer starts the process 24 months in advance, and the average internet lead requires 12-15 touches before a client responds (some industry experts say more). The average agent stops following up after two or three tries.[1]

Here is a success hint: the money is made between the 5-12 touches.

Some more disturbing facts about our industry … also according to NAR:

- 49% of email leads NEVER receive a response
- 51% of text inquiries NEVER get a response
- 29% of phone calls NEVER get a call back (when they are returned, it takes an average of one hour and forty-

---

1 "Research Reports." *Research and Statistics*. National Association of REALTORS®, n.d. https://www.nar.realtor/research-and-statistics/research-reports.

five minutes after the initial call).[1]

If you are in a market that has ibuyer programs available to consumers, you may want to try asking for an instant offer on your home (via Opendoor, Offerpad, or Zillow) to see how quickly they respond.

Then ask yourself: are you delivering content like that as quickly as they are? The answer will probably be no.

These disruptors in the marketplace know the flaws in our industry, and they are kicking our butts with quicker response times and more consistent follow-up. A lead is an opportunity until the buyer/seller tells you to pound sand.

Dominating the real estate market requires that we become good stewards of data and facts. Know your conversion rates; know where your leads are coming from; study your numbers and study the numbers for your market. Be honest about how good you really think you are, and then find a way to up your game.

Set a measure of success for yourself daily, weekly, monthly, quarterly, and yearly. The best way to move the ball forward is progress, not perfection.

One of Nate's favorite quotes is: "Everything works, and nothing doesn't."

Put a different way: don't be afraid to try something new or different. Just because no one else is doing it in your market doesn't mean it won't work.

> *Part of success is failing, and without failure, we would never know what success is.*

Relationship-based Selling

One of the most brilliant listing appointments Sarah ever had the privilege of attending with Nate was so simple, yet it was extremely powerful and did not require a flashy listing presentation. For that matter, there were no comps or marketing examples.

---

[1] ibid.

Sarah Says …

The owner, a widowed elderly woman, had lost her lifelong mate a few months prior, and the house was just too much for her to maintain. We toured the house and then sat down at her kitchen table. Nate asked her two questions: "Janet, what is your goal, and how can we help you get there?"

Which leads to the next realization by Theodore Roosevelt:

People don't care how much you know unless they know how much you care.

We never talked with Janet about property values or how we planned to market the home. We never discussed commission or how great our team was. No, we listened to her story, helped her uncover her goal, and prioritize her immediate needs. When we walked to the front door to leave, she said, "Send me your listing agreement and tell me what you think we should list the house for."

We should add that we sold her house plus an investment property and helped her son buy his first house, too. Again, people don't care how much you know unless they know how much you care.

☙

Being a strong listing agent requires that you know the data, that you study the market, and that you have tools to expose the home to a large pool of potential buyers in a polished and professional way (which is the Multiple Listing Service, by the way). But the most important skill you must develop is the ability to make people feel like you care about their needs and that you will help them prioritize their goals. If they like you and they trust you, they will do business with you—and then (assuming you do a bang-up job, they will refer you to their family and friends).

Just like baseball, the game of real estate is all about the number of times you get on base (for our purposes, the face-to-face appointment). You *can* dominate any real estate market if you consistently get on base every time you are at-bat.

Recap Step Six: You Can Win a Baseball Game Hitting Singles, But the Only Way to Know if You Are is to Track Your Stats.

You can go online at REM.AX/TRACKERS to download a sample tracker for lead generation, lead conversion, open houses, lead tracker, and the Top 50 tracker.

If you have been implementing the concepts we have taught you so far, your business is on its way to dominating your marketplace—good job! Let's keep that momentum going with our playbook on how to create lifelong raving fans—in the next chapter!

- 10 -
Our Tell-all: How to Create Raving Fans

"Make the customer the hero of your story."

~ Ann Handley

One of the best ways to lead gen with your Top 50 and/or database is through client appreciation events. To really knock it out of the park, if you want to engage your database, plan 6-8 events throughout the year where prospects are face-to-face with you.

While we don't want to date the content in this book with current world affairs, we would be remiss if we did not touch on the global pandemic. Despite what is happening, people are still buying and selling homes, and no matter who is in the White House, they still need help with their primal need for shelter.

Our industry is resilient and innovative. Agents across the world have found unique and creative ways to remain top-of-mind with their clients, despite mandatory quarantines and state-wide shutdowns of non-essential businesses.

As you read through this chapter, please keep an open mind on how you can take these ideas and make them socially responsible to safely engage your database throughout the year.

If you are new to the industry or have never done a client appreciation event, just start with one event and keep adding each year. There are literally hundreds of ideas for client appreciation events, but we thought we'd share some that we have tried and some that seem to draw the biggest engagement.

Before we dive into the event ideas, let's look at the real power of the database touch that comes as a result of hosting one of these events. You speak to your database (these are the touchpoints) multiple times while planning your event. That is the real power of the event—the several times you are in contact with people before and after the event. Even if the people you invited don't show up, you still made the touch.

Step Seven: Get Face-to-Face with Your Database as Often as You Can.

In reality, only a few people will show up at your event. Depending on the type of event you are planning, that's okay, and here is why. Let's say you have 300 people in your database; they all get the invite. Most don't attend, but they appreciate being invited. However, one touch was made through the initial invitation. If that contact does RSVP yes, you give them another touch when you confirm their plan to attend.

Before the event, you call to remind them and answer any questions. That's an additional touch. Now, they get their photo taken at the event in front of your branded backdrop (RE/MAX balloon, Tube Dude, or logoed banner)—by the way, using a branded backdrop pulls additional attention to you from other consumers who are not in your database. That is another way to "squeeze the orange."

After the event, you send your contact a copy of the photo from the event, whether that is digital, print, or on social media (which should include a hashtag that everyone uses to drive your brand awareness). This is another touch with your client.

We hope you can see that hosting a client event has multiple opportunities to engage and touch your database over and above anything else we do in marketing. Now let's have some fun and talk about some great ideas for hosting a client event!

Movie Events: Pick an appropriate movie for your database and make sure you rent the theater on opening day or weekend (this is a critical detail; otherwise, you may not get the same engagement). Big blockbusters like *Star Wars* or any Marvel movie will be well-attended—as will family-friendly Disney movies. If it's a movie containing superheroes of popular characters, you can take it up a notch by "renting" an actor (like Superman or Batman, for example). Then allow your guests to take photos with the character. This is a great way to "wow" your database!

We took the movie idea in another direction a few years ago and hosted an adults-only premiere of *Bohemian Rhapsody*. We had "concert" style-tees made and encouraged our clients to dress up in their favorite music genre. We also provided a little more food than a typical movie theater might and served adult beverages. There were no print invites for this event; we focused our efforts on direct calls to our Top 50 and filled the theater. It was a smashing success, not to mention a fun time!

We also hosted the last *Toy Story* movie and turned it into a toy drive to benefit our local Phoenix Children's Hospital. The beauty of a movie event is the ease of planning, as you can leverage the national marketing the theaters are already doing. It is relatively low cost, and you can parlay it into other community-driven benefits. This is a highly effective way to touch a lot of your database without a lot of time in planning or cash out-of-pocket.

Another spin on movies is renting a drive-in movie theatre. This is a great idea for an event that could still occur during a pandemic. People would be physically distanced but engaged with you at the same time. If your city or community does not have a drive-in theatre, consider renting an inflatable screen and hosting your movie night at a community park. If you have a farm area, that makes for an entertaining community event that will engage your farm database.

Sporting Events: If you have a major league sporting team in your area, taking a Top 50 to a game creates a more personal one-on-one experience. This is the thing about sporting events: you don't need the tickets to make the touch. We used to get on the phone and call a bunch of past clients and invite them to a Diamondbacks baseball game that day. The majority of people would say no because it was last-minute. But even if they couldn't go, people were extremely appreciative of the thought and invite. If someone does say yes, buy the tickets. Even better, buy yourself a ticket and go with your client to the game.

A few years ago, Nate attended a charity auction event and bid on a game night at the Diamondbacks in a box suite. This was a double win because he was able to support a local charity with his winning bid, and he deepened the relationship with a small group of his elite Top 50 with a private suite—talk about "squeezing the orange!"

In the past, we have hosted spring training baseball games, but they never got a ton of great engagement, mostly due to the time of day. While spring training is huge in Arizona, we were not paying attention to the fact that the majority of our database was at work on a Wednesday at 1:00 pm. A spring training baseball game is an excellent touch as there are only two states that host games. Obviously, this won't work unless you live in Arizona or Florida—but if you do, then it's a great idea because nobody else can offer it. If you are going to offer this benefit, make sure you pick an evening or weekend game time to get better engagement.

A client event needs to make sense for your database, and that is why a variety of events throughout the year will get you the most engagement across different lifestyles, personalities, etc.

Holiday Open Houses: Hosting a holiday event is a classic touch for any database, and it's an easy time of year to engage your Top 50. Don't plan it too close to the holiday and make it easy for people to attend. Your database will look forward to getting the invite every year. These types of events can be hosted in your own home (if appropriate), a local restaurant, or at your office—if there is space for a party.

Thanksgiving Day Pies Give-Away: Almost every family in the U.S. celebrates Thanksgiving Day, and a pie is a great way to show your appreciation. However, delivering hundreds of pies to your database is not the highest and best use of your time. Instead, consider hosting a "reserve pop-by." This is an event at your office or local pie business where your clients come to you. Make it a party with light appetizers and hot cider or adult beverages.

If you aren't comfortable hosting an indoor event but love the idea of giving away a pie, you may consider doing a "drive-by pie giveaway." This is sort of like picking up your groceries from your local store or Walmart. Your clients could still come to your office, but instead of coming inside, they simply "drive through" to get their pie. You place it in their back seat, or trunk and voila! The touch has been made.

Here's a helpful tip: Costco has the best price for the value on pies, and people love them. Also, make sure to support your local businesses if you can.

Photos with Santa: This is another idea that can be turned into a party with food and beverages for your clients to enjoy. To provide even bigger value, invite not only the kiddos but their four-legged friends, too!

Happy Hours: This is an easy way to get started with client events. They are reasonable in price (depending on where you host) and don't require a lot of setup to successfully pull off.

One of the teams in our office does a quarterly birthday event; their Top 50 is invited to have a drink—on the team—each quarter depending on when they had a birthday. If there is more than one person in a household (and there usually is), that is an additional touch they get to make because the spouse/partner will attend both happy hour events. These are great ways for agents to use birthday data and engage some people in their database that were otherwise stagnant.

Annual Shred-Events: An annual shred-event is a clever way to engage a farm area if you are working one subdivision or community. One agent who works for a brokerage started a shred-event in the community where she lives and farms. It was so well-attended last year that she had to hire a second truck to accommodate all the neighbors who showed up. She does a great book of business right in her own backyard. In recent years, she has parlayed her shred-event into a charity affair by taking donations to benefit our local Phoenix Children's Hospital.

Monthly Marketing: Every month throughout the year has a big holiday, except the month of August. But don't despair; there is a website called NATIONALTODAY.COM that has a calendar of all the whimsical "National Day" holidays that can be used for a little inspiration. Remember, too, at the end of Chapter 8; we provided you with a great base of monthly marketing ideas that you can implement today. Be sure to bookmark that chapter if you haven't already.

Community or Local events: If there are big community or city events in your area, you can leverage their marketing efforts to engage your database. For local events like summer festivals, fall festivals, holiday events, etc., give your clients tickets to attend. To take it to the next level, create a hashtag that your client can use on social media to let people know they are attending the event because their REALTORS® gave them the tickets.

Drives: Any kind of "drive" can be effective, too, and depending on where you live, essential for your community. Some ideas include blood drives, coat or hat drives, food drives, and toy drives. There are literally hundreds of ideas you can turn into a well-received client event. The important goal is seeing your Top 50 or the people in your database in person—consistently throughout the year.

Get Involved in Your Community: Nate is great at community involvement and supports a variety of charities, groups, organizations, and businesses, like women's shelters, the Phoenix Children's Hospital, the Peoria Center for the Arts (Theaters Works), 1Life Fully Lived, etc. One of our favorite teams in California (Amalfi Estates) donates 10% of every commission to one of five local charities (the client gets to pick). They cover the bases with organizations that benefit homelessness, children, health, and animals. Since 2014, they have donated more than $1 million to those charities. They are changing lives in their community.

Our brokerage participates in the Children's Miracle Network program, and we are proud to share that after every closing, a significant amount of our agents donate to our local Phoenix Children's Hospital. For the past several years, each August, we have taken our fundraising efforts up a notch by participating in the RE/MAX "Month of Miracles," which involves raising money throughout the entire month. Our brokerage has donated more than a half-million dollars (and growing) since 2001, and that is something we are really proud of!

Typically, we host weekly fundraising events throughout the month, and our final push is a big live auction event at the end of the month that contributes to the majority of what we raise during the Month of Miracles. Well, this year, because of the pandemic, we had to get creative—as we didn't want to change our goal of $20,000 that we were planning to give to the Phoenix Children's Hospital. So, we took to a virtual stage.

Our change in plans worked because we are blessed to have an amazing agent in our ranks, Rick Ramirez, who just happens to be a singer in a local band—Throwing Fitz. We approached him about hosting a "virtual concert," sort of like an old-school Jerry Lewis telethon! We weren't sure how it was going to turn out, but we forged forward in unchartered territory, and while we didn't smash any numbers, we did end up raising over $20,000 in August 2020—despite the pandemic! #REMAX4KIDS

> *Get involved with organizations or services that you believe in.*
> *Give to the people in your community.*
> *Give to your client's kids.*
> *Give to your church.*
> *Give to the schools.*
> *Give to the shelters.*
> *Give to the veterans.*
> *Give to the homeless animals.*

But don't do it for the business; do it because you like it and are passionate about it. Make a difference in the community you serve, and the result will be more business.

When we talk about our involvement with PCH/CMN, it is rare to meet someone who hasn't been touched by the services they provide to the kiddos in our community. And because they see how passionate we are about giving back; it makes them want to do even more business with us.

Our involvement with PCH started twenty-five years ago with a charity golf tournament that was held at Arrowhead Country Club in Glendale, Arizona. It was pretty amazing when we got the news that PCH will be building a hospital in our backyard, and we can't help but feel that our donations helped to contribute to the hospital's ability to grow and add additional services for our clients and community. #REMAX4KIDS

Planning Client Events: To host 6-8 events per year requires strategic planning in advance. Look ahead at the year and put the dates in your calendar now. Create a checklist of everything you will need to do to execute a successful client event and a list of those who can/will help you. Don't throw everything together at the last minute. That is a huge waste of money, and you will be disappointed with the outcome. Make it a priority to plan it in advance. Depending on the type of event, you need, at a minimum, thirty days to promote it to your database (but sixty is better).

Don't be afraid to ask your vendor partners to help with the cost, planning, promotion, and day-of tasks. If you are giving them business, they are making money, and so, they are usually happy to support your business—especially because it means they will get more of it. If you are new or have a limited budget, you can host an event with a couple of other agents that you trust and share the expenses with them. The client won't know who is there; they will only care that they were included.

One of the keys to a successful client event is how you communicate with your database. There are five prongs to this communication:

- Phone call
- Text message
- Video
- Email
- Facebook Messenger

Be where your clients are online and make it easy for them to connect with you.

Last year during our Month of Miracles event, I tested Facebook Messenger with our agents. It was a few days before our big live auction event, and only thirteen people had RSVP'd on our company Facebook page. With a little effort, copying and pasting the event link and private messaging our agents, we went from thirteen to more than thirty in just twenty-four hours—plus, we received two additional donation items for the live auction. This all happened because we made it easy for people to say yes or no to the invite.

A phone call is still the most powerful form of communication, with email being the least preferred form of communication for most people. Interestingly, Facebook Messenger trumped text messages and came in as the second-best way to communicate with clients; even if they are not active on Facebook, the Messenger app is used by a large audience.

The goal is to host 6-8 client events per year, which requires planning, a budget, and tracking. Make sure you have a sign-in sheet for all your events to collect updated information (like phone numbers and emails). You can use the sign-in sheets to track who is showing up to your events and if they prefer one type of event over another. You also have the opportunity to engage your attendees with a follow up to thank them for attending, which can be in the form of a phone call, a handwritten note, or if you had photos taken at the event, you could have them printed and sent out in an inexpensive frame (remember the concept of "squeezing the orange?").

The agents we coach who are delivering well-executed client events are getting referrals—*every single time* they host an event.

Recap Step Seven: Get Face-to-Face with Your Database as Often as You Can.

Want to take your marketing plan to the next level of accountability? Share it with our private Facebook group! Just search **8 Ways to Dominate Any Real Estate Market**. See you there!

- 11 -
Accountability = Love

"If you do what you've always done, you'll get what you've always gotten."

~ Tony Robbins

The final step in dominating any real estate market, and we saved the best for last ... is accountability. We have found that accountability is like hearing the word "homework" when you are in sixth grade. Our hope is that by the time you finish this chapter, you will have a shift in your perspective because accountability = love.

Step Eight: Find a Mentor or Accountability Partner, Hire a Coach, and Never Stop Investing in Yourself.

Three success principles accompany the topic of accountability:

1. Find a mentor or accountability partner,

2. Hire a coach, and

3. Invest in yourself.

Let's unpack these a little more.

Find a Mentor or an Accountability Partner: What is the difference between a mentor and an accountability partner? Mentors show up throughout our lives and might range from our first teacher in elementary school to our favorite coach in high school sports. Nate's first mentor was the legendary Howard Brinton, who he met by chance at a GRI (Graduate, REALTORS® Institute) class in Tucson, Arizona—which ironically ties to the third principle of investing in yourself.

If Nate had not invested in himself by getting his GRI designation, he might not have met Howard, his first real estate mentor and a man who impacted his life professionally and personally. Nate learned from Howard to "Get out of judgment and into curiosity," which caused him to see the world through a different lens. That resulted in setting bigger and bigger goals that he never dreamed could be achieved. It was all due to one guy who didn't want anything but to help him live his best life.

> ***This is the difference between being a mentor and having an accountability partner.***

Howard Brinton's career went far beyond that of just a GRI instructor. You might even remember the group Star Power, which was comprised of a group of elite REALTORS® Howard put together to share their success. He hosted events across the globe and included specialized seminars for teams and buyer agents where "Stars" would share how they became the top producing agents.

Nate recounts, "I was a part of that elite group of "Stars," and in 1997, we happened to be in Cancun for a Star Power event with Dr. Fred Grosse as one of the presenters when I was first introduced to the term 'accountability partners.'

"I was sitting next to my dear friend and fellow 'Star,' and when the speaker suggested that we look around the room and pick an accountability partner. My friend and I picked each other. The extent of our 'accountability' was making sure the other one was okay when we saw each other at the next real estate event. Now, there were two other agents attending the same conference who didn't know each other, but from across the room, they made eye contact and did the 'man nod' to confirm their pick as each other's accountability partners.

"Those two gentlemen were Pat Hiban and David Osborn. At the time, Pat was a Star Power Stars as well as a top agent in the industry; in fact, Pat was the number one RE/MAX agent. David was a guy in the audience who got in on the man nod; however, he was on his mom's team, which happened to be one of the first Keller Williams teams.

"Fast forward 20+ years, and those two individuals have become wildly successful, multi-millionaire REALTORS®, bestselling authors, and nationally known speakers. They, along with Tim Rhode, are also the founders of an amazing accountability group known as GoBundance™. These men took accountability to a whole new level and the result today is their massive success—not just in real estate but in life. If you don't know who they are, Google them. Then buy their books."

&

Whether you are new to the industry or a seasoned vet like us, find a good mentor or accountability partner who will help you grow yourself and your business. Be mindful that your accountability partner can actually hold you accountable. It will do you no good to make another friend who buys into your stories for failure; a good accountability partner holds your feet to the fire and doesn't let you off the hook with an excuse.

We base our success and our future goals on what we have done in the past. So, find someone who will be brutally honest with you, especially when you need to be called out on your own B.S. Find someone doing it bigger and better than you, someone who challenges you to be the best version of yourself, someone you can trust and who can help you see the bigger picture, as well as someone who challenges you to get out of judgment and into curiosity. Through them, you will learn what you are really capable of. As Howard would say, "Write down how much money you want to make. Now draw a line through it and double it!"

&

> **"Deliberately seek the company of people who influence you to think and act on building the life you desire."**
>
> **~ Napoleon Hill**

Speaking of legendary accountability, in 1925, author Napoleon Hill coined the concept of mastermind groups, and since then, thousands of lives have been changed. If you don't have a one-on-one mentor or accountability partner, consider joining a solid mastermind group. Within our brokerage, we have several masterminds designed for different levels of production, while others focus on how to invest in real estate.

※

In Nate's Words ...

A few years ago, I was invited to join GoBundance™, a tribe of healthy, wealthy, generous men choosing to lead epic lives, founded by none other than David Osborn, Pat Hiban, and Tim Rhode. I had been invited to join before, but to be honest, I was intimidated and way outside my comfort zone. The way that some of these guys defined success made it sound like their goals were in another dimension! But I am glad I did join, as GoBundance™ has been really instrumental in taking my career and life to the next level.

It's through this tribe that I met a guy named Jim Campbell. That led us to open Title Alliance Professionals, which is our title company share-owned by our agents. Launching this business was an opportunity for us to create a passive stream of income for our agents while also enabling us to provide the quality of title/escrow service that I expect our clients and agents to experience.

Had I not joined GoBundance™, I may not have crossed paths with Jim, and so, I might never have opened Title Alliance Professionals. Which is a good reminder that we are the average of the five people we spend the most time with—and for me to compare who I was surrounded by forty years ago to who I am today is freaking incredible. Being among leaders has made me a better leader, and by constantly raising my game, I have changed the people I lead. #MINDBLOWING

When I look at all these events, people, and decisions from a bird's eye view, I can see how the dots connect and how one person changed my life. While he is no longer with us, there is not a day that goes by that I don't think of my dear friend and mentor, Howard. He singlehandedly changed the lives of countless people, the Stars of the organization, and future generations of family members, team members, and industry leaders.

Everyone he met, he changed.

Sarah is the dynamic instructor she is today because Howard saw something in her and invited her to step out of her comfort zone to lead her first break-out session at a Star Power Conference. She was also invited to be among the elite cadre who taught the 3-day Team Training for Star Power, which continues to be a significant highlight (and privilege) in her career. I have no doubt that I would not be the man I am today if fate were to have it any other way, and I never crossed paths with Howard. And we are not alone. Anyone who met him would wholeheartedly agree. He was one of the greatest influencers in our industry and continues to live on through each of us who had the honor of knowing him. I cannot thank him enough.

Howard was the catalyst that set the course of my career and the existence I am blessed to live today, which affords me the opportunity to make a difference in our industry, in my community, in my family, and to impact the lives of those agents I am proud to call RE/MAX Professionals. Thank you, Howard.

> *"Really, coaching is simplicity. It's getting players to play better than they think that they can."*
>
> *~ Tom Landry*

Find a coach: In the beginning of your real estate career, you may not be able to afford a top-notch coach. But make it a goal to get there financially as quickly as you can. Over the years, we have invested in several coaching programs to help our team as well as the brokerage, and to this day, Nate has coaches.

Keep in mind that not every coach is the right coach for you, and it might take going through a few coaches before you find the right one. One of Nate's first coaches wanted him to knock on doors and pound expired listings—he hated it—which resulted in Nate rebelling against him. Don't just hire any coach; you have to find the right coach for you and your business.

A good coach will take a helicopter view of your business and allow you to see what you might not be able to. It's true; we get so caught up in our day-to-day tasks that we lose focus of our goals because we are too busy managing the deal or the team. A good coach cares about you and is invested in your success, which means they will hold you accountable for what you say you want out of life. It doesn't matter if that pisses you off, makes you cry, or scares the crap out of you. Because accountability = love.

A good coach is only half of the equation; the other half is you and your willingness to be coached. You must know the answer to the question: *are you coachable?*

It is not easy to let someone point out weaknesses or call us out on our excuses. It is not easy to openly listen to someone else's perspective, especially when we have been doing something "our way" for years. Being coachable requires you to be vulnerable, and that can be painful, uncomfortable, messy, and scary. Did we mention uncomfortable? Being "coachable" means you are willing to try new things, create fresh habits, break through limiting beliefs, and trust that you don't have all the answers or even have to know all the answers. It means that you know it's okay to ask for help.

Both of us are Master Coaches for Workman Success Systems based in Salt Lake City, UT. We met co-founder Verl Workman more than twenty years ago when we invited him to do some training for our agents in Glendale, Arizona. That was our first experience with Verl's genius, and we fell in love with his gregarious energy and unstoppable determination.

Over the years, we have watched his company develop into what is now one of the leading coaching companies for real estate agents, especially teams. Like Howard Brinton, Verl shares the same passion for the real estate industry and has a drive to make a massive difference in the lives of agents across the country. We'd like to take this opportunity to say thank you to Verl for taking the road less traveled and for having a vision that we are both so proud to be a part of. If you'd like to learn more about the training, tools, services, and coaching that Workman Success Systems offers, please reach out to them at workmansuccess.com.

Invest in yourself: Nate remembers that there used to be a publication called the *AAR Trade Journal*. One day, as a new agent, he saw an advertisement for the Tommy Hopkins Boot Camp.

As he puts it: "I can still see it clear as day in my mind – there were two army boots and a helmet—and it cost $299 to attend. I went to my broker, advertisement in hand, and I asked him if he would pay for me to go. I told him I would sit in the front row and come back and make both of us a bunch of money. He laughed at me."

Nate realized at that exact moment that if he was going to be anything in real estate, he would have to back himself. No one else was going to.

"I was working in construction when I got my license. I had no self-esteem, no self-worth, arms covered in tattoos that I was embarrassed by, and I certainly had no business sense. I'd made some bad decisions so far in life, and construction was the best job for a guy like me, especially because I worked on Mel's crew. To be on Mel's crew was the best because he was like the Michael Jordon of construction, and there were only ten of us. Mel ran the concrete team, which was made up of a hierarchy of guys who made better pay and who were respected on any job site. If you were on Mel's crew, you were the big shit!"

Nate knew if he was going to build his confidence, he needed to get some designations. He believed that if he had a few letters behind his name, he would be a "legit" REALTOR®. But to get his first designation, the GRI, he needed a week off work (that is how they did GRI classes then).

It must have been kismet because Nate learned about the GRI designation in the same publication that advertised the Tommy Hopkins Boot Camp. The message of education and personal development kept coming to him. Which is a good reminder to never give up on developing yourself—that you are your own best investment.

But at that time, Nate had a problem.

He remembers: "In construction, time is money, and I had a coveted spot on Mel's crew that I could be risking by asking for time off. But I also had a belief, and to honestly support that belief, I had to be all-in, which meant risking my steady paycheck and benefits. If you are going to risk it all, you have got to be all-in and believe in the outcome. I asked for the time off."

Mel was one of Nate's greatest inspirations as a human being. When he asked for the week off, Mel said to him, "If you can get out of this business, I will give you the week off."

"Mel gave me the confidence I needed to take the next step in my career."

That was his first learning experience at a GRI class in Tucson, Arizona and his instructor was none other than Mr. Howard Brinton.

Howard was the first real estate instructor who Nate ever met in this type of formal learning environment (after quitting college). To say Howard's stage presence was dynamic is an understatement. There are just no words to truly describe his charisma, his wit, his charm, his ability to capture the audience in a way that made you laugh, cry, and get on your feet from sheer inspiration. He was hands-down the best, and Nate was hooked on education from that day forward.

"That day is still crystal clear. I remember being uncomfortable, shy and a bit lost. Then it got even more uncomfortable when we were asked to get up from our seats and hug ten people in the room—ten random *strangers*! I was never hugged growing up and had never hugged another man in my life.

"I never had any male affection, and Howard filled that void for me. He made me feel good about myself; he made me feel special. Which had nothing to do with selling real estate.

"Howard taught me a valuable lesson: you are who you are, and don't ever be embarrassed to be who you are. He walked his talk, too. Everywhere he went, he left a giant impact, which is a good lesson for all of us to remember. You leave a trail wherever you go, and you have an opportunity to make a difference, whether that is good or not. We can all be a little bit like Howard, leaving the world a better place than we found it.

"If I had not met Howard that day in Tucson, I don't know that I would be here today writing this book. I owe him a debt of gratitude I will never be able to pay."

The GRI designation behind Nate's name gave him an edge and a great foundation for his real estate career.

Nate's thirst for knowledge never changed even after achieving his ABR, CRS, GRI, e-PRO, CDPE, CIAS, CLHMS, CRP, and SFR designations.

Let's unpack a few of the reasons why Nate chose these designations.

Accredited Buyer Representation (ABR) – Before this designation came to be, we worked under a unilateral sub-agency agreement meaning that it didn't matter what brokerage you worked for; we all represented the same seller leaving the buyer to beware. When the Multiple Listing Service decided this wasn't the best way to protect either party in a real estate transaction, the rules were changed, which meant that now we could exclusively represent a buyer. Nate has always pushed to be ahead of the curve, not only to be the best in the industry but to be able to provide the best experience for his clients.

Certified Distressed Property Expert (CDPE) and Certified Investor Agent Specialist (CIAS) - These designations were rolled out during the distressed market to teach REALTORS® how to successfully navigate the short sale transaction (CDPE) and how to represent investor clients who were looking to cash in on those opportunities (CIAS). Almost everyone on the team earned these designations. It was a way to pivot in the rapidly changing real estate market while continuing to be at the top of our game.

Certified Luxury Home Marketing Specialist (CLHMS) - When Nate wanted to move into the luxury home market, this designation was key to building creditability with luxury homeowners and opened the door into that market with peers and industry leaders. It's a pretty impressive and difficult designation to earn and definitely holds value in the luxury industry.

For Nate, designations were a way to gain confidence and stand out in public. He did not get the endorsements or accolades from his father, and designations were the replacement for that missing part of his life. As he grew as a REALTOR®, designations were important to stay ahead of changes in the industry, to acquire knowledge, and ultimately to better serve the client.

For thirty-five years, Nate has made it a point to attend as many real estate learning events as he can. He has been to everything from National Association of REALTORS® conventions to the CRS Sell-a-bration, and Tom Ferry, Mike Ferry, Brian Buffini, Ken Goodfellow, Alex Charfen, Verl Workman, and Gee Dunsten events, to name a few. You could say he is a bit of a seminar junkie, but he wouldn't be who he is without the influence of so many incredible industry leaders.

Nate has also been to the annual RE/MAX convention (R4) every year since joining the brand because he believes strongly in the power of education. He says: "If you are not learning, you are dying, and a thirst for knowledge should never be quenched." FYI, he still sits in the front row!

"Knowledge is love and light and vision."

~ Helen Keller

Nate has shared his drive for knowledge with our brokerage through the creation of a program called Pays for A's. This program is for the students in our RE/MAX Professionals family. For every A grade they earn, we give them $5.00, and at the end of each semester, their names are entered into a drawing for a big prize, usually an iPad. Education is one of Nate's core values, and through this program, our company makes an impact to change lives and the future of our community.

Invest in yourself because, in most cases, no one else is going to do it for you. Get the designations. Take the classes. Go to the conventions. Hire a coach. Join a mastermind, and don't stop reading new books.

Top performers across the world share a few facts in common: they attend 6-8 personal development events each year, and they have a coach (most even have more than one type of coach).

They also consistently invest 10% of their income into their personal development. If you are making $100,000 annually, that is an investment of $10,000. If you are a million-dollar earner, then you should invest $100,000 into yourself. We are here on this earth to live our life to the fullest, and that requires us to remain learning-based no matter how many homes we sell, how much money we make or how many goals we check off the list.

> *"You are one decision away from a completely different life."*
>
> *~ Mel Robbins*

Our final thought as we conclude this chapter surrounds the word "action." All the best practices in the world, in any industry, are worthless without action. All the knowledge and skills will get you nowhere without action. The best coaches, books, and seminars are wasted without action. To truly be learning-based requires a commitment to mastery. It is the act of not only learning but *applying* massive action over and over that achieves success.

Recap Step Eight: Find a Mentor or Accountability Partner, Hire a Coach, and Never Stop Investing in Yourself.

If you are ready to hire a coach, we'd love to have a conversation with you about what Workman Success Systems has to offer and why we are Master Coaches with their organization. Send an email by visiting 8WaystoDominateAnyRealEstateMarket.com.

In Closing ...

- 12 -
The Future of Real Estate

"The future's so bright, I gotta wear shades."

~ Timbuk 3

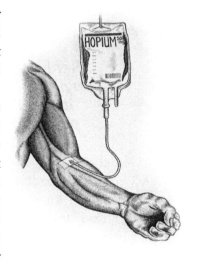

Before we dive into the final chapter and our thoughts on the future of real estate, let's talk about some important data when it comes to today's online lead generation.

In 2011, there were 4.5 million online leads generated and 4.8 million homes sold. Just a few years later, in 2017, those numbers jumped significantly to eighty-six million online leads and 5.5 million homes sold. The following year, in 2018, there were eighty-nine million online leads generated and 5.9 million homes sold, which means there were 80.3 million more leads paid for by REALTORS® than homes sold![1]

When we take a deeper look at this data, this is what we can learn from it ...

In 2020, over 100 million online leads were generated. Out of those leads, 42-45% of those inquiries NEVER got a response from an agent. Twenty-three percent got one response or less. For an industry that spent $13 billion in advertising in 2020, this is a shocking and disappointing statistic to discover.

Let's go even deeper to where the money is made.

Online leads take relentless follow up. Most agents are great at

[1] *"The Lead Response Management Study." **LeadResponseManagement.Org**. InsideSales.com, n.d. http://www.leadresponsemanagement.org/lrm_study.*

generating them but suck at consistently following up – almost half of leads don't even get a call back. A mere 12% of agents make it to a third contact. That number shrinks to 10% for those agents who follow up beyond three touches. But that is where the money is made–in follow-ups 5-12.

REALTORS® have become addicts to lead aggregators like Zillow, BoomTown, Commissions Inc., etc. And all those big online gen companies are selling you what we like to call "Hopium."

Sadly, REALTORS® across all markets are also spending big money they often don't have on leads because they "hope" they will make them money—yet they're not even following up with them according to the National Association of REALTORS®!

As Nate says ...

> *"Real estate is the hardest, high-paying job you will ever have, but it can also be the easiest low-paying job you will ever have."*

It is your choice.

Nate went from spending thousands of dollars a month and attracting leads that he didn't know to spending that same amount of money on people who already knew and trusted him.

If you are reading this book, and you don't have those people and closer relationships yet, heed this important tip: never forget that the people you meet every single day are the ones who can impact your business in the future.

The future of real estate, and more specifically, *your* future in real estate, depends on the quality of the relationships you have with your database and your SOI. Once again, these are the people who know you, like you, and trust you. Agents who can master these relationships will continue to be in business at a consistently high level. While those who focus on chasing online leads because they are addicted to "Hopium" could find themselves pursuing other career fields.

☙

> *"The purpose of a business is to create a customer who creates customers."*
>
> ~ Shiv Singh

Find Your Niche and Master It

You have to find what works for you in real estate as you also find your gifts and understand what you are good at—and what you are not good at. That's not to say you should avoid what you are not good at—especially if it's vital to your business, but you can choose to surround yourself with people who can fill the gaps of your deficiencies.

It's also imperative that you learn to delegate. You are not the only one who has all the answers or knows the best way to accomplish a real estate task. Trust us on this one!

We have surrounded ourselves with an awesome team of talented people for many years because we learned to delegate. You can't scale your business until you learn to delegate. And while we are talking about delegating, hire your first assistant (besides your children) as soon as you can afford to pay that person. Remember the little trick we mentioned earlier: if you can't afford someone right now, consider aligning yourself with a real estate brokerage that offers transaction coordinator services. For a flat fee per transaction, you can have an assistant who is already trained and experienced.

For over a decade, our agents at RE/MAX Professionals have had the highest production per agent in the state of Arizona. We believe the secret sauce of their results is that we have taught them to delegate to our in-house transaction coordinators.

> *"Minds are like parachutes – they only function when they are open."*
>
> ~ Thomas Dewar

Find Your Unique Value Proposition

Don't get caught up in the office water cooler gossip: "That won't work in my market." That is a limited thought disguised as an excuse.

Be bold.

Be daring.

Think about Jeff Hoffman, the guy who invented Priceline.com. His boss told him that he'd never make it.

Think about how online travel has forever been changed because he had a vision and the courage to go after it, despite the criticism (remember that he also became a billionaire doing it).

What about Michael Jordan, who didn't actually make the varsity team in high school? That didn't stop him from going on to become one of the greatest basketball players of all time. Multi-Grammy winner Lady Gaga was told she had no talent by her teacher. She has gone on to influence the entertainment industry and thousands of little girls, who are now inspired to follow their dreams. What if she had given up because *one* person told her to?

We are all born with gifts, talents, and abilities that change the world, and we have an obligation to share them. There are countless inspirational stories like these—are you one of them?

> **"You don't have to be great to start,
> but you have to start to be great."**
>
> *~ Zig Ziglar*

The real estate industry is amazingly innovative and resilient because we, as a collective whole, are constantly learning and adapting. While the basic components of a real estate sale are typically the same, no one transaction is alike.

In 2019, Nate decided to purchase a Motto Mortgage franchise, which required that he attend training at RE/MAX World Headquarters in Denver. While he was there, he got an offer on a house that he had listed on the street where he lived.

It was a full-price offer with a two-year lease-purchase contingency. Nate was in a class learning about mortgages, which caused him to start asking questions he might not have asked if he hadn't been learning about the mortgage process.

Long story short, Nate ended up orchestrating the deal and got the buyer approved for a loan, even though they had been told they didn't qualify. This resulted in four families served, and four REALTORS® paid, all from one piece of knowledge that Nate learned.

Another idea coined by Jeff Hoffman is info-sponging. This concept involves not only learning something new every day but keeping a log or journal of everything you learn over time. We want to challenge you to make it a goal to learn something new every day and to keep a daily journal of what you learn. Then never give up on the pursuit to become the very best version of yourself that you can be. The future of real estate depends on it; your future depends on it.

Lastly, allow us to offer this advice: if you are a top-producing team, stay a top-producing team.

If you want to be a sales manager, be a sales manager.
If you want to be a broker/owner, be a broker/owner.
If you want to be a recruiter, then be a recruiter.
Just don't try to be ALL of these positions.

Nate has no regrets; however, his career and business decisions have required a tremendous amount of work and sacrifice. Massive responsibility comes from trying to fulfill all those roles in one brokerage. He has spent many sleepless nights trying to keep all the machines operating.

"Watch your thoughts; they become words. Watch your words; they become actions. Watch your actions; they become habits. Watch your habits; they come character. Watch your character; it becomes your destiny."

~ Frank Outlaw

The Pandemic in the Real Estate Industry

This chapter is titled The Future of Real Estate, and again, we don't want to date this book, but we *have* to touch on the current pandemic and how it is impacting the industry.

Never in the history of the world has such an event shut down the entire planet, and we have no way to predict the repercussions of this in the next year or even in 5-10 years.

Some businesses are struggling, while others are flourishing.

Some businesses have realized they can't work from home, while others have successfully figured it out.

Will office space be as relevant post-pandemic?

Will more ibuyer-based real estate companies emerge?

Will we see a reduction of agents in the industry?

Only time will tell.

What we do know for sure about the future of real estate is that there will continue to be innovators who are pushing for more technology and better, more streamlined ways to execute a real estate transaction. The demand for more technology will be stronger than ever, and the virtual experience is not going away post-pandemic. The drive for video has been a topic for years, and the pandemic has forced many of us to finally embrace it. Technology is not a replacement for human touch in a real estate transaction; rather, it's a tool to help you create an amazing experience for your clients—one that deepens the relationship and creates raving fans for life.

The future of real estate always comes back to one thing: mindset. Mindset is everything, whether the market is good or bad, whether there is low inventory, too much inventory, a pandemic raging, or an election year. Mindset is what gets us through the challenges and what creates new opportunities.

Use your mindset to get outside of your comfort zone. Push yourself to do one more call, one more open house, and knock on one more door – until that is your new normal.

Realize, too, that the market is good or bad, depending on your mindset. Whatever you believe it to be, is what will materialize for you.

We have lived through every type of market over the last 30+ years, and we are here to tell you all about it because we chose to focus on the right mindset, which kept us innovating, adapting, and moving forward.

Have the right mindset and focus on the right money-making activities every single day, and you will have a profitable long-term future in real estate that will pay you tenfold for decades to come.

☙

As we conclude this book, let's recap the *8 Ways You Can Dominate the Any Real Estate Market*, Regardless of Market Conditions.

Step One: Get Crystal Clear on Your Big Blue Dot. If you don't know your true big "why," you will struggle with the how. Both are vital to succeed in any business, especially real estate.

Knowing your "why" at a cellular level will help you get out of bed on the days that you'd rather hit snooze because a deal fell through, or you lost a buyer to another agent.

Living your B.H.A.G. every day will push you to places you've only dreamed about. Your "why" is your north star, your rally cry. That is why it is Step One. You have to start here to dominate anything in life, including real estate.

Step Two: Create a Business Plan and Working Budget.

This is where the rubber meets the road, and you put your blue dot into action.

When a goal is written down, it is proven that it has a better chance of being realized. Don't gloss over this step—get clear and then put it in writing. If you don't have access to the documents you need, remember, we created a journal called *Your Real Estate Journey to Abundance: 8-Step Journal* to help you, and we also want to invite you to join our private Facebook group, where we can hook you up with everything you need in the industry.

Step Three: Create an Intentional Week and Put It Everywhere. Get intentional about what you are neglecting in your life and business. Identify your big rocks (like date night with your significant other or the gym, and don't forget about prospecting–yes, it's a big rock!). Then build a calendar you can commit to weekly. Remember, time is the only limit we have, and for every yes, you are saying no to something else. To dominate the real estate industry requires an intentional and focused commitment to how and where time is spent. Mastering this step will create more time and leverage in both your business and life.

Step Four: Identify the Top 50 People in Your Life Who Love You, Trust You, and Have Either Done Business with You or Would if You Asked Them To. Then love the heck out of them as if your life depends on it—because it does! Make it a goal to get a referral from every person in your Top 50 each year. If you can do that, you will never wonder where your next sale is coming from.

Step Five: Create a 12-month Written Marketing Plan, Implement, and Execute Consistently. Remember, everyone knows another agent, so sending one holiday card is not enough interaction with your peeps to keep you top-of-mind throughout the year. We gave you a ton of great ideas in Chapter 8, and that is not the end-all-be-all list of ideas. There are thousands of affordable ways you can connect with those people in your database, and here's a little tip: they want to hear from you!

Step Six: You Can Win a Baseball Game Hitting Singles, But the Only Way to Know if You Are is to Track Your Stats. Then use the data you discover to make improvements in your business. If something isn't working, kill it. Don't be afraid to stop using a strategy that is not producing the results it should so that you will have a stronger ROI. And don't be afraid to be bold, unique, and try something that no one else is doing. That is the most important thing we can do as a collective industry; it is how we innovate and ultimately deliver the best experience for the consumer.

Step Seven: Get Face-to-Face with Your Database as Often as You Can. Raving fans are people who are evangelical about you. They go beyond just liking and trusting you to represent their next real estate transaction. No, these folks transcend that and rise to another stratosphere. They are the lifeblood of a thriving real estate practice. The best way to create raving fans is through face-to-face, personal interactions like pop-bys or client appreciation events. Make it a goal to get in front of your raving fans at least once a quarter so you can continue to maintain and develop the relationship. Raving fans keep you fat and happy.

Step Eight: Find a Mentor or Accountability Partner, Hire a Coach, and Never Stop Investing in Yourself. Remember that accountability equals love, and if you love your business, your clients, your community, your family, and yourself, then accountability is a must. Doing this is a high level of personal commitment to growth and development. It's hard at first, messy in the middle but freaking amazing at the end. Your family will thank you; your business will thank you, and your life will thank you.

✦

We'd like to invite you to check out our companion project to this book.

As we have both shared our powerful experiences through using journals to create massive change, note the importance of tracking every aspect of business, stay top-of-mind, have a budget, and record daily accountability—we have designed a journal specific to the eight concepts we have shared with you in this book.

We have also included a daily journal so you can hold yourself accountable to doing the tried-and-true money-making activities. Do this with a high level of consistency, and you will dominate any real estate market. Purchase a copy of our journal: ***Your Real Estate Journey to Abundance: 8-Step Journal*** at: REM.AX/YOURREALESTATEJOURNEYTOABUNDANCE.

AFTERWORD

The book you've just read is the summation of a 30-year business approach that anyone can master. As Nate and Sarah Michelle make it clear throughout, there's nothing magical or overly complex in the strategies that helped them build their business.

Of course, being capable of executing a strategy isn't the same as actually doing it. That's where Nate and Sarah Michelle stand out. They've put in the time, learned from incredible coaches, and done the work—over a span of many years. As they note toward the end of the book:

> *"All the best practices in the world, in any industry, are worthless without action. All the knowledge and skills will get you nowhere without action."*

Action is what matters. And taking action requires planning, delegation, and prioritizing (so you have the time) as well as the resolve, consistency, and fitness (so you have the energy).

If you're at an earlier stage in your real estate career, I hope you noticed the action behind the ideas being shared in these pages. For instance, Nate didn't just believe in professional development; he took the classes and earned the designations. Sarah Michelle didn't just plan for the team being so visible in the community; she organized events and made it happen.

In the end, real estate is a relationship business. It's about skilled professionals—armed with the best tools, systems, and technology of the day—taking action to connect with people and help them achieve their real estate goals. The whole RE/MAX network is built on that notion.

Nate Martinez and Sarah Michelle Bliss grabbed the premise and ran with it. In fact, they're both still going strong—and in many ways are better today than ever before. Now, through this book and more, they're helping other professionals find their way, too.

That, to me, is a success story.

Adam Contos
CEO
RE/MAX Holdings, Inc.

ACKNOWLEDGMENTS

We'd like to acknowledge the following people and organizations for their contribution to our business, our success, and our lives.

To the thousands of families, friends, and clients we have served over the last three-plus decades, thank you for your trust in us as your real estate confidants. We are better REALTORS® and human beings because of you.

The amazing leadership at RE/MAX Headquarters. Thank you, Dave Liniger, the Southwest Regional team, Adam Contos, and Nick Bailey. We are surrounded by greatness, and that is why nobody in the world sells more real estate than RE/MAX.

Thank you to Verl Workman for your dedication to making the real estate industry even better than it already is. We appreciate your vision, hard work, and passion.

To the team members, past and present, "Thank You" barely begins to scratch the surface of the profound gratitude both of us have for every single one of you who we have had the privilege to work next to in the trenches. You rock!

Our amazing, talented, dedicated, selfless, loyal crew who keep the wheels on the bus at RE/MAX Professionals, thank you. Please know we could not do what we do without your passion, support, and commitment.

With much gratitude to our families for the many late dinners, sleepless nights, and their "ride or die" commitment, love, and support. You are the reason we could write this book.

And lastly, to one of the greatest men to ever walk the earth, Howard Brinton. There is no doubt we would not be the people we are today without his massive contribution to our lives, both professionally and personally. May you forever rest in our hearts and memories. Thank you.

ABOUT THE AUTHORS

Nate Martinez, REALTOR®, Broker/Owner, Team Leader, Master Coach, Author, Coach, ABR, CRS, GRI, e-PRO, CDPE, CIAS, CLHMS, CRP, and SFR

Nate Martinez is the owner of RE/MAX Professionals, a multi-office franchise located in the greater Phoenix area. The highlight of running his business and team is getting to work in the trenches every day with the love of his life Tonya, his oldest daughter Brandi, and his son Nate Jr.

Nate passionately believes in the value of education, having trained hundreds of real estate professionals across the globe as a speaker and a coach. With more than thirty-five years in the real estate industry, he has been recognized with the Lifetime Achievement, Titan Team, Circle of Legends, and the Luminary of Distinction from RE/MAX. He is most proud of the charitable contributions of his agents to the Children's Miracle Network and their support of this organization. In addition, he is proud to be ranked the number one brokerage in Arizona when it comes to production per agent.

Outside of work, Nate enjoys golfing and spending quality time around the pool with his adult children, Nate Jr., and Brandi, his confidant Tonya, their daughter, Mila, and three grandchildren.

RE/MAX Achievements:
Hall of Fame 1995
Lifetime Achievement 1999
Chairman's Club 2002, 2003, 2004, 2005, 2006, 2007, 2008, 2012, 2014,
Platinum Club 2001
Circle of Legends 2006
Diamond Club 2009, 2010, 2011, 2013
Diamond Club Team 2017, 2018, 2019, 2020
Titan Club 2015
Titan Club Team 2016
20 Year RE/MAX Anniversary 2011
25 Year RE/MAX Anniversary 2017
Luminary of Distinction 2017

Sarah Michelle Bliss, Master Coach, Author, Speaker, Real Estate Trainer, ABR, e-PRO

For almost twenty-five years, Sarah Michelle Bliss has been a part of the RE/MAX family and an original founder at her brokerage in sunny Arizona, RE/MAX Professionals. She joined the number one Nate Martinez Team as a buyer's agent in 1997, and in 2002, took the position of team leader to manage Nate's team for the next ten years.

She is a published author, has trained both locally and nationally, including for the development and delivery of accredited real estate classes.

Sarah is a Master Coach for Workman Success Systems based in Salt Lake City, UT, and a certified DISC/Motivators Practitioner, Star Power Speaker/Trainer, licensed REALTOR®, and author for RISMedia. Today, she is the Director of Agent Development and teaches the RE/MAX Momentum Complete Agent Development Program™ for her brokerage.

DISCLAIMER

The content of this book is based on the authors' decades of experience in the real estate industry and has been carefully crafted to be intended as a source of information only. The authors and publisher assume no responsibility or liability for any damages or losses that may be incurred during or as a result of the implementation of the concepts and ideas contained herein.

The suggestions and materials provided in this book do not constitute legal or other professional advice. You should consult your professional adviser for legal or other advice in regard to accounting, finances, taxes, fees, or any real estate-related costs or expenses. All information written is for educational and informational purposes only.

Past performance may not be indicative of future results, and results may vary from reader to reader depending on the application and commitment to the use of the content herein.

Made in the USA
Las Vegas, NV
02 August 2021